Archives
and
Local History

Archives
and
Local History

F. G. EMMISON

MBE, DU(Essex), FSA, FR Hist S.,
formerly County Archivist of Essex

PHILLIMORE

First published in 1966 by
METHUEN & CO LTD
11 New Fetter Lane, London, EC4

Second edition published by
PHILLIMORE & CO LTD
Shopwyke Hall, Chichester, Sussex

1974, reprinted 1978

Printed in Great Britain by
UNWIN BROTHERS LTD
at The Gresham Press, Old Woking, Surrey

Preface to Second Edition

I would like first to thank Phillimore & Co. Ltd. for inviting me to prepare this revised edition, and at the same time to express, as others would wish me to do, appreciation to its Hon. President, Dr Marc Fitch, F.S.A., F.R.Hist.S., from whom so many authors and editors of works on English local history have received financial assistance towards the cost of publication through the Marc Fitch Fund in the past 18 years.

Acknowledgements
and References to Sources

The author's grateful acknowledgements for supplying illustrations and extracts are due to the Local and Episcopal Authorities or Trustees and to their Archivists or Librarians in charge of the following Local or Diocesan Record Offices or Manuscripts Departments of City Libraries; also to the Private Owners, Incumbents and Parochial Church Councils who have deposited so many of their archives in public custody. *Plates* in italics; extracts in roman type.

COUNTY RECORD OFFICES: Bedfordshire, *9*(a) [Q/SM 1]; Buckinghamshire *25*(a) [microfilm]; Cambridgeshire *24*(a) [R 59/31/19/5/2]; Cornwall 7 [Basset MSS.], 19 [D.D.X.1/1]; Derbyshire 15 [D. 166]; Devon 24 [380A/H2]; Dorset 4 [P47/SU1]; Durham 3 [EP/W: 17]; Essex *title-page* [D/P 166/8/2], *1*(b) [Q/SR 146/34], 23 [D/P 30/13, 30/14], *tailpiece* [D/DU 65/86], 5 [D/P 156/8/2], 7 [D/P 202/13], 8 [D/P 156/8/1–4], 9 [D/ABW 55/219], 20 [D/TE 1, 2], 25 [EML 51/1]; Glamorgan *13*(b) [DDSF320], *20* [D/D G 1836(1, 3), 17 [D/DF]; Herefordshire 16 [Davenport MSS. B47]; Hertfordshire *13*(a) [QS Misc.976]; Kent *9*(b) [P.S./Se 1], *31*(b) [CTR858B]; Lancashire *11*(a) [QSB/1], *31*(a) [AE/7/7], *32* [PDC/25, PDR/132, PDB/11], 18 [DDX/28/299]; Greater London *2* [P92/SAV/591], *6*(a) [P92/SAV/1358], *24*(b) [M.B.W. 1584]; Monmouthshire *12*(b) [Hanbury D.8.114]; Northamptonshire *15* [Fitzwilliam (Milton) 2099, 2112]; Nottinghamshire *6*(b) [QSM 12], *30* [DD.HO 1/6]; Oxfordshire *26* [Wi. VI/iv/26]; Shropshire *18*(c) [122/21], *28*(b) [81/599]; Somerset *17*(b) [D/P/She 13/1], 12 [D/DSP], 21 [G/BW 8(a)/1]; Staffordshire *3* [D.593/S/4/18/6], *4*(a) [Lichfield R.O., B/V/1/55], *12*(a) [D.1734/3/3/212]; East Suffolk *19* [Acc. 276/172], 22 [50/13/113, HA12/B4/29/40]; West Suffolk 10 [Ac. 592, 1/45]; West Sussex *4*(b) [Ep. I/26/2], *28*(a) [Petworth MS.], *29* [Goodwood MS. E30]; Warwickshire *11*(b) [QS 40/4]; Wiltshire *17*(a) [A4/4/2]; Worcestershire *21*(b) [b705:24/381 (6a)], *27*(b) [b736 BA 2006/10/83]; Yorkshire, East Riding 23 [LBW/1, 2].

[ix]

ACKNOWLEDGEMENTS

CITY AND BOROUGH RECORD OFFICES AND MUSEUMS: Bristol *10* [04273(1), 00205(1)], *14*(a) [04352(5)], *21*(a) [AC/JS/36(2)w]; Chester *8*(b) [Charters 49A]; Gloucester *8*(a) [Glo.Char. 1/2]; Guildford *1*(a) [BR/OC/1/2]; Leeds *16* [MC185, KF1/3, MC134], *18*(b) [SM 22/1], *25*(b) [TN/C9]; Liverpool *14*(b, c) [352 MIN 1/5, Kf 96]; Nottingham 13 [M2359]; Waltham Forest (London Borough) *18*(a) [L 47]; Westminster 2 [E.40], 6 [F.5003].

OTHER REPOSITORIES: Borthwick Inst. of Hist. Research, York *5* [R.VI.A.14, R.IV.N.65, R.IV.F.1792/1]; Prior's Kitchen, The College, Durham 11 [Prob., Cons.Ct.Dur.]; Shakespeare's Birthplace, Stratford-on-Avon 1, 14, 22.

OTHER OWNERS: R. B. Verney, Esq., *25*(a); The Most Hon. The Marquess of Anglesey, *3*; Corporation of Wardens of St. Saviour, Southwark 2; Vicar and Churchwardens of St. Cuthbert, Bedford *27*(a).

I wish to thank Mrs N. K. M. Gurney and Mr E. Welch for advice on ecclesiastical and borough records and Mr [now Dr] F. W. Steer and Dr F. Hull for reading the whole draft; errors that remain are of course my responsibility. I am also grateful to Professor A. G. Dickens for help and criticism.

Contents

CONTENTS

* *not listed, but fully indexed*

[xii]

Preface

Discovering and reading local archives is of absorbing interest. To many it is a leisure-time pursuit – finding out more about the history of one's county, town, village, or maybe one's Tudor cottage; tracing the rise and fall of a local industry or craft; piecing together the first biography of an active Commonwealth J.P. or a successful Georgian clockmaker, or searching for one's own ancestors and learning some surprising facts.

In recent years a new and apparently insatiable demand for historical records has come from universities, colleges and schools. Thousands of teachers and students are flocking into local record offices and libraries with manuscripts. They are researching for a higher degree or undergraduate essay; finding maps and surveys for a surveyor's or architect's examination; collecting data for a College of Education special study; searching for local material to enliven the teaching of national history; undertaking group study of a collection of records in an extra-mural or Workers' Educational Association course; looking for the first time at original documents and being encouraged by their interest to follow up a topic for a school prize essay (secondary grammar and modern schools are rapidly realizing the possibilities).

This book has been written for both categories of reader, amateur and academic. Frank Herrmann, a director of Methuen & Co., who lives in an historic manor-house in Essex, knowing that I was the pioneer county archivist in developing facilities for the use of records especially for educational purposes, asked me to compile something after the style in B.B.C. booklet, *Introduction to Archives* (1964, revised edition, Phillimore, 1974), but in more detail.

Despite the wealth of material provided, it has not been extended to include medieval documents, because they give rise to many difficult problems. The starting point is around 1538, when parish registers were instituted. On the other hand, I try to explain how to make relatively light work of the Latin and the handwritings of sixteenth- and seventeenth-century documents.

The emphasis is almost wholly on *local* records in *local* repositories, as most readers will have little opportunity to examine archives in the national repositories in London, Oxford, Cambridge and Aberystwyth, the contents of which are of course more complicated and cannot be described in a book of this size. Although county (council) record offices have shown the greatest expansion in recent years, the student should not overlook the wealth of material in city and borough record offices and those big city libraries which have old-established departments of manuscripts.

Everywhere facilities for students, advanced and beginners, are growing – more printed guides and catalogues, more indexes, more exhibitions. These ease the task of those who wish to consult the records. But such guidance to students depends largely on staff. Some of the older record offices are fairly well staffed, but others may be limited in their facilities by staff quite insufficient in number to cope with the multifarious duties of the local archivist. (Before any collection is made available, hundreds of hours may have been spent in searching for and negotiating its deposit, and in arranging, classifying, repairing, numbering, boxing, cataloguing, typing, and indexing by subjects, parishes and persons; in addition to which basic work the archivist is expected to prepare exhibitions, give lectures, answer postal inquiries, deal with committee and administrative duties, and perhaps also to take charge of vast quantities of modern records of his local authority or help in the reference department of his city library.)

Staffs of county and borough record offices generally form part of the departments of the Clerk of the County Council or the Town Clerk, because the primary duties of the archivist are with the official records. The astonishing growth recently in use of records by universities and colleges of education and by schools is of only indirect concern to the County or Town Clerk, because he is not responsible for education. If therefore a college principal or head teacher feels that the reasonable needs of his staff or students are not being met by a local repository, probably because of understaffing, it would be appropriate for him to seek the support of the Chief Education Officer in recommending the Clerk to ask for some improvement. (It should be added that some County and Town Clerks for many years have given most influential support to archivists, while some Education Officers have not yet realized how many educational facilities archivists provide.) The plain fact remains that the big growth in the use of archives for educational purposes has not led to a corresponding increase in the archive staffs responsible for meeting these demands.

It is necessary to enlarge a little on this aspect, though much of what follows is only my own view. University students, trainee teachers and senior school pupils will be taking up a lot more of local archivists' time in the near future. To a small minority of my profession, with many other pressing demands, these inroads on their limited time are unwelcome. I am not among the minority, but the position has become serious and urgent action is required. A chief criticism is that some students arrive without adequate tuition. A few university supervisors, college lecturers and schoolteachers admit that they have little time to give it. Others frankly do not bother, hoping that the keenness of the archivist will supply it. This is not good enough. Most archivists are indeed keen, but the specialist help needs to be recognized at higher levels, instead of its being taken for granted.

In the Essex Record Office, which probably has the highest student attendances among local offices, the position recently led to my presenting a report on assistance to university students. As this would also apply with suitable modifications to trainee teachers and schoolchildren and as the subject is of general interest, a few extracts will be given. The controlling committee was told that help, often over a period of years or almost daily in some months, included:

Answering initial postal inquiries (some lengthy) about subjects and sources, and later inquiries after the student had ceased to attend.

Discussion at first interview with the supervisor of the students' room or other member of the staff, when the student made his exploratory survey of the subject and its possible link or clash with that of others in the same field.

Suggestions for suitable sources to clear specific problems arising in the course of research.

Help in reading and interpreting difficult documents.

Advice on secondary works of reference of local significance.

Advice on the local context of problems.

Help based on individual archivists' specialized knowledge of the contents of the repository or of particular classes or on their knowledge of the subject, topography or families derived from their personal research.

Advice on illustrations, reproductions, and editing.

Yet, in the opinion of a distinguished director of historical research, 'it should not be necessary for local archivists to explain to post-graduate students in history how to use the records produced for their inspection'. However much I agree with this view, theory and practice do not coincide too well. After being in close touch with them for over thirty years in two county record offices, it is my considered opinion that local archivists who have a proper knowledge of their archives and area, adequate understanding of British political, social and economic history and historical geography, and some experience in research and publication are especially well qualified to give advice parallel with that which the student receives from his academic supervisor. The results of much research would be the poorer if this were not freely offered. My report also stated:

> A number of researchers who do not have the benefit of seminar instruction (as at London) have declared that the discussions in office and after-office hours with the senior staff have been most beneficial to them, not only for the practical information received but also for psychological reasons – the relief from what can be the lonely isolation of research, often undertaken far distant from university contacts, with little opportunity for exchange of ideas or discussion of problems.

Mr E. K. Timings, in an important article, 'The Archivist and the Public',[1] written in 1962 when he was in charge of the literary search-room of the Public Record Office, was equally emphatic about 'the significance in the changing role of record offices, which are becoming more and more adjuncts of the Universities . . . All this is very legitimately within the archivist's province . . . probably he alone could have given the necessary guidance'.

If the Universities and Colleges of Education wish that our help should continue undiminished, some form of tangible assistance towards the provision of extra staff is required. Preliminary steps were recently taken in this direction (an encouraging start), but if influential support is not forthcoming quickly increasing demands may seriously jeopardize students' needs. This would be regrettable and is avoidable. In advance of corporate recognition on a national basis by universities and colleges, much could be done by them on a local level in helping archivists to provide the facilities needed by their students.

[1] *Journal of the Society of Archivists*, April 1962. The subject was pursued in my article, 'Local Record Offices and the Universities' (*History*, liv, 1969, 229–33, supported by the Editor). Many useful suggestions from archivists as to unexplored subjects are in *Material for Theses in Some Local Record Offices* (ed. F. G. Emmison and W. J. Smith, with a foreword by Professor A. G. Dickens, Phillimore 1973).

I

Aids in using Local Archives

Introductory

In recent years innumerable treasures enriching the history of all parts of England and Wales have been discovered through the energetic efforts of members of a new profession supported by several national bodies, by public-spirited county and town councils, local societies, and by private owners and custodians of local records. Beginning in one county (Bedfordshire) and one city (Bristol) less than fifty years ago, there is now a county record office in almost every county and in most of the larger ancient boroughs, staffed by qualified archivists. They have classified, catalogued and indexed the official records. They have searched for and secured countless archives from a variety of sources and have made these manuscript riches available to everyone. And this incredible wealth of material is rapidly increasing, as more and more historical documents come into public custody.

Maps, wills, inventories, deeds, registers, letters, diaries, account-books, minute-books, pictures, handbills, and many other kinds of fascinating records have been secured. They tell in more or less vivid detail the story of every place and every family. They afford new material for almost every conceivable subject of local interest:

The land – including agriculture, the open-field system, commons, greens, heaths, enclosures, crops, implements, gardens, parks, forests.

The sea and the coasts – including ports, docks, wharves, piers, fisheries, ships, smuggling, lighthouses, cliffs, marshes, manuscript charts of coasts and creeks and oyster-layings, coastal defence, beacons, wrecks.

Communications – including roads, footpaths, bridges, ferries, rivers, canals, floods, coaches, turnpike trusts.

Crafts, trades and industries, their rise and fall; their visual relics in town and country (whether scenic or architectural) such as millponds, or water-mills, smithies, shops, market-crosses; or objects like furniture and clocks.

Buildings, from castles, abbeys and mansions to farm-houses, cottages and barns; mills of many types, factories, guildhalls, almshouses, workhouses, inns, schools (King Edward VI, so called, dame, day, Sunday, British National, Board and so on); and churches, with their bells, monuments and plate. Of course churches, almshouses and schools are material aspects of the much wider subjects of religion and nonconformity, poverty and charity and education.

Crime and punishment, gaols, stocks, justices of the peace, police.

Health, sickness, plagues and fires. Food and drink. Sports and pastimes.

In past ages archives were often kept for safety in treasure chests or deed-boxes. Consulting archives in a local record office in pursuit of topics such as those just listed is not unlike opening any of three imaginary chests inscribed SUBJECTS, PLACES and PERSONS. The keys to these chests are the indexes provided by the archivist in charge. The quest may be for material, say, about the bridges on a certain river. The Subjects index-key unlocks the first chest and reveals a small partition labelled 'Bridges', which in turn yields, maybe, copies of a Chancery case concerning liability for the repair of one bridge, letters from the architect of another bridge, and the original building contract for a third bridge on the same river. The Places chest contains many partitions, one for each parish in the county through which the river runs. Several of these parish units reveal an estate map with a detailed drawing of one bridge, an antiquary's dated sketch of the oldest bridge on the river, and an early and rare engraving of another, pulled down and rebuilt in 1740. Finally, using the index-key to the Persons chest, the searcher, to whom the names of the architects of two of the bridges is known, discovers new biographical details about them.

Or the search may be for material relating to a group of adjacent villages in the Civil War and Commonwealth period. The keys may give access to taxation lists showing the sums assessed on each parish towards maintaining the Parliamentarian forces, to a parish register recording civil marriages published in advance in the market-place and performed by local J.P.s, to facts about their activities in Quarter Sessions and in other ways during this abnormal period.

Such are a few of the signposts (for that is what indexes are) to inviting avenues through which the quest may be followed. But it would be wrong to suggest that all avenues are simple to traverse. Some indeed, tempting at first sight, may prove to be mazes instead of avenues. But a maze challenges, and the solution which will lead to the end may justify the effort in finding it.

In this book we shall explore avenues and mazes which are not beyond the capacity of the amateur. We shall not examine medieval manuscripts, which demand difficult techniques (though the beginner may later on be inspired to master some of them). We shall restrict our examination to local records dating from about 1538, when parish registers were instituted. It is an arbitrary date, though useful, because there was a big increase in the making of local records, ecclesiastical and civil, official and private, after the Dissolution of the Religious Houses. Many estates – those of the 'new men' of the Tudor age – appear, or re-appear, under secular ownership, with the surrender of the monasteries.

Some post-medieval manuscripts, especially those of the sixteenth and seventeenth centuries, may appear at first to be dark, overgrown avenues unless the explorer's equipment, in addition to his general knowledge, includes at least one tool and one torch of the right sort. The former may be needed to cut a path through Latin stretches; the latter to illuminate apparently indecipherable handwritings. To furnish himself with these two aids, post-medieval Latin and Palaeography (the study of old handwriting), is definitely not beyond the reach of the amateur with a little determination and a little leisure. Give it a trial.[1]

Latin

Although most Tudor, Stuart and slightly later local documents are in English, the fact remains that the language used in many legal records of the local as well as the central courts was Latin until 1733. By a Commonwealth ordinance all legal records were to be written in English (they reverted to Latin at the Restoration), so that 1653–60 is an 'easy' period. With that exception, it means that the formal proceedings of the county justices in their Courts of Quarter Sessions, of borough courts, manor courts, bishops' and archdeacons' courts and the like are mostly in Latin before the date when it was finally superseded by English (1733). It means also that many other local records, such as parish registers, title deeds, leases and so forth are in Latin, though such less formal documents as these tend to be written in English long before 1733.

[1] A prize, endowed in 1945, for Essex school pupils' essays based on study of original records, was intended to encourage simple research, and has proved conclusively not only how much pupils can gain from the experience, but what a useful contribution some of them can make in a small way in the field they choose to explore.

But those to whom this may seem to be a barrier may be assured at once that it is probably a lower obstacle than first imagined.

1. The Latin used in such documents is infinitely easier to learn (and translate) than classical or even medieval Latin.

2. The scribe thought in English and so the construction of the Latin sentences is very simple in comparison with classical Latin.

3. It is consoling that many scribes' Latin was limited and they resorted to English when stumped, using a general Latin word followed by *anglice* (meaning, in English) and the English term, e.g. *tunica anglice* jerkin.[1]

4. Court records, deeds and other local records employ phrases which are used with such frequency and regularity as to be readily recognizable after a little study.

5. Familiarity with these phrases in post-1733 (or somewhat earlier) documents in English eases the reading of the same phrases in Latin.

6. There are useful reference books and cribs.

In addition to the ordinary Latin dictionaries the reader will probably need to consult two standard books, *The Record Interpreter*, by C. T. Martin (its sub-title is 'a collection of abbreviations, Latin words and names used in English historical manuscripts and records') and *The Medieval Latin Word List*, revised (1965) by R. E. Latham; both should be available in any good public library.

For home study, *Latin for Local History*, by Eileen Gooder, is useful for the beginner. It contains exercises and many hundreds of typical phrases used in local records, together with 'A small formulary of some common Latin documents met with amongst local historical records: namely gifts, bonds, powers of attorney, fines, quitclaims, manor and borough court rolls, accounts, and some typical ecclesiastical records'; these are mostly medieval examples with translations. The forty-six page dictionary in the appendix is a selection from the two preceding works and although limited it provides an adequate vocabulary for the amateur local historian. *Village Records*, by John West, also gives a short but very useful glossary of Latin words commonly found in local archives.

Local documents in Latin with full translations of the sort most

---

[1] Two more examples from indictments in the Essex Quarter Sessions rolls, 1676: (1) 4 men publicly vexed a vicar reading the Book of Common Prayer, '*tonitruendo cornua anglice* bloweing theire hornes', and (2) an oyster-dredger entered '*unum linterem anglice* a skiffe' lying in another man's oyster-laying and stole a peck of oysters (E.R.O., Q/SR 432/45, 46). Some scribes tried valiantly to put up a show of classical Latin. Shakespeare ridiculed them in '*honorificabilitudinitatibus*' (*Love's Labours Lost*, V, i), a word which has indeed been found in York diocesan act books (J. S. Purvis, *Introduction to Ecclesiastical Records*, 12).

frequently met with (e.g. court records and deeds) are available in print in many books, especially the publications of local record offices and historical societies. *Village Records* gives a five page list, arranged by counties, of printed manorial records.

Examples of the simple, coined Latin words often met with in local archives are *certificatio* (certificate), *comitatus* (county), *vicecomes* (sheriff, literally viscount, vice-count), *messuagium* (messuage, dwelling-house), *sursumreddere* (to surrender), *veredictio* (verdict). Likewise, the present-ment of a road out of repair, describes it in a Quarter Sessions or manor court roll as *ruinosa, confracta, in magno decasu* (in great decay), or *lutosa* (muddy), marking the mire into which classical Latin had sunk. Most early parish registers were nominally written in Latin, but there is no difficulty in recognizing the few words for 'were married', 'twins', and so forth.

Handwritings

If medieval and Tudor handwritings are to be thoroughly understood and mastered for the proper examination of records of English history, the study of palaeography should begin with the beautiful Caroline minuscule and then proceed with concentrated attention to the peculiar 'set' hands of the Courts of Chancery, Exchequer, King's Bench and Common Pleas, the 'legal' hand, the 'bastard' hand, and gradually extend to the 'secretary' or last of the Gothic and cursive hands. The early Tudor secretary hand soon had a rival in the imported italic. But the latter, from which our present writing has descended, did not finally vanquish the secretary hand until after 1700.

However, having regard to the restriction of our present study to local documents of post-medieval date, little is needed beyond an under-standing of the relatively easy 'secretary' handwriting of the sixteenth and seventeenth centuries. Many scribes of Latin and English manu-scripts before about 1700 made little or no distinction between the strokes of 'm', 'n', 'u', and 'i', each stroke being called a minim (the word itself consists only of minims), or were careless (as we still are) in dotting each 'i'. If in doubt, count the number of minims and try several likely permutations. The writer, the first Bedfordshire archivist, once noticed John Bunyan's name written as thirteen identical minims spelling 'Bunniunn', but the Latin *minimum* beats that by two minims. Look at Plate 10(b), last but one word of line 7 and Plate 3, line 16.

The commonest abbreviation is for 'per-' or 'par-' (horizontal stroke through stem of 'p', see Plate 5(b), lines 2, 3 and 12, 'parish', personn[es]' 'parte', and Plate 9(a), line 9, 'apperes and imparles').

The contraction for 'pre-' (flourish above line after 'p') is seen in Plate 6(a), middle of line 11 ('prepared').

The contraction for 'pro-' (stroke through stem of 'p' brought round from above) is seen in Plate 6(a), last word of line 15 (provided') and Plate 9(a), last line ('protest').

By about 1600–50, 'par-' ('per-'), 'pre-' and 'pro-' were usually written in full, but Plate 6(a) has examples of each in both abbreviated and extended form.

Another method was to leave out part of a word and note the omission by putting above the line one or more letters from the part omitted. See Plate 11(a), lines 1, 2, 3, 5 and 8: 'y^e' [for 'the'], 'wor-[*shi*]pps that', 'w[*hi*]ch', 'offend[*e*]r'; by the sixteenth century one of the two Old English characters for 'th' had become indistinguishable from 'y', hence the special contractions for 'the', 'that', 'this'. Never transcribe words ending in '-cion' as '-con', as is too often seen in print (see Plate 10(a), lines 8, 9).

The standard 'teach yourself' book for the amateur historian reading local records is Hilda Grieve's *Examples of English Handwriting, 1150–1750* (Essex County Council, 2nd edn., 1959), containing thirty plates, with annotated transcripts and translations of Essex local archives. In addition there are now two Historical Association pamphlets, K. C. Newton's *Medieval Local Records: A Reading Aid* (1971) and F. G. Emmison's *How to Read Local Archives, 1550–1700* (3rd edn., 1973), each with a dozen plates and annotated transcripts.

Golden rules for copying a document written in a difficult hand (and these apply equally to modern or present-day writings!) are:

1. Begin with common words such as 'the', 'and', 'if', 'with', 'for'.

2. From these and other words the reading of which cannot be in doubt construct your own alphabet by writing out the letters in fac-simile, noting how the strokes were made, remembering that there may be two or more forms for certain letters, such as long and short 's'.

3. When in difficulty, refer to your alphabet.

4. Don't guess. (The writer nearly slipped up when reading what seemed to be a very common saint's name in Plate 7, line 2!)

5. If your reading produces a strange word, you (not the document) are probably to blame.

6. Be ten times more careful if you intend to have your work printed!

Some Helpful Books and Journals

Before tackling almost any subject demanding or inviting consultation of old archives, some general knowledge of it is usually needed. Obvious as this should be, experience shows that many people, especially young students, tend to read manuscript records before reading the essential printed books. Occasionally, a preliminary glance at manuscript material may help in determining if it is suitable or adequate for detailed study, but, with few exceptions, background reading should come first if the student has not already a sufficient knowledge of the topic. This applies equally whether it is concerned with political, social, economic, religious, military, maritime, or other aspect of national history, or whether a local aspect is to be studied; and of course almost every subject associated with local history requires some knowledge of national history for its intelligent study.

In recent years many books, pamphlets and journals have given real help to those about to tackle local history and local archives. The *English Local History Handlist* (Hist. Assoc., 3rd edn., 1965) is an invaluable guide to a large number of books and articles. In 1962 the same Association's journal, *History*, began a regular four-page series of 'Short Guides to Records'. In each article a transcript of, or extract from, a typical document such as a probate inventory is followed by practical notes and a very short bibliography. (They are listed in the Appendix.) The Standing Conference for Local History (National Council of Social Service) has published several useful pamphlets (see the Appendix). *The Local Historian* (formerly *The Amateur Historian*), published quarterly by the Standing Conference, has included since 1952 many articles of the utmost help to beginners, as the *Subject Index* (1966) will reveal.

Trainee teachers and senior school pupils should not fail to study *Local History Essays: Some Notes for Students*, by R. Douch and F. Steer (University of Southampton Institute of Education), and *Guide for Research Students working on Historical Subjects*, by G. Kitson Clark (C.U.P.), although intended for the university student, offers much practical advice generally.

Local Records: their Nature and Care (ed. L. J. Redstone and F. W. Steer for the Society of Archivists, 1953) has chapters on the main groups of records and a useful bibliography.

If the reader is living near one of the larger public libraries he may also find it helpful to ask for the publications of the British Records Association comprising pamphlets and its journal *Archives*, which

includes detailed accounts of nearly all the older local archive repositories, and the *Journal of the Society of Archivists*, containing articles
on numerous classes of local records; but these journals are not for
the beginner. R. Somerville, *Handlist of Record Publications* (B.R.A.)
gives examples of archives, arranged under headings such as manor
court rolls, which had been printed before 1951.

No student of local archives should fail to consult the volumes
(where published) of the *Victoria County History* and the *Inventory*
volumes of the *Royal Commission on Historical Monuments* (churches and
buildings before 1714), also the county volume of the English Place-
Name Society, *Buildings of England* (ed. N. Pevsner), both series now
covering half England, *The Making of the English Landscape* (ed. W. G.
Hoskins, general vol. and vols. for Cornwall, Lancashire, Gloucestershire and Leicestershire, 1955–7), and *The New Survey of England* (ed.
J. Simmons, vols. for Middlesex and Devon, 1953–4). If he is concerned
with any aspect of local topography he should absorb all he can from his
one-inch or six-inch Ordnance Survey maps (old and new editions).

The Historian's Guide to Ordnance Survey Maps (N.C.S.S.) is an invaluable pamphlet. And as a change from poring over manuscripts he can
then get into the open air and visit his area (or, if living there, view it
afresh), especially if he has also read W. G. Hoskins, *Local History in
England*, J. Finberg, *Exploring Villages*, M. Beresford, *History on the
Ground*, F. Celoria, *Teach Yourself Local History*, or J. B. Mitchell,
Historical Geography.

A 28-page pamphlet *Introduction to Archives* (revised edition, 1974, by
the publishers of the present book) is also devoted, but in somewhat less
detail, to post-medieval local archives and has forty-six illustrations of
various types of document most frequently used by students, with
transcripts or translations of some of them. In considerably more detail,
and furnished with many examples of records but few illustrations, is
Sources for English Local History (1973), by W. G. Stephens, who provides
an extremely large number of references to other books and articles.

Especially helpful is *Village Records* (1962), by John West, new edition
due 1975, drawing wholly on Worcestershire archives. It contains many
illustrations with Latin or English transcripts. As its name implies, it
excludes archives of towns but students of urban archives will find much
to help them. Although the main examples are centred around a single
village, the book is useful to all students of local archives because of its
long lists, referred to again later, of books and articles for each county
on quarter sessions, manorial and other records.

There are also source-books, each containing hundreds of extracts

[8]

from local records but without illustrations, for two other counties. Kent County Council has issued a series entitled *Kentish Sources*, viz. *Some Roads and Bridges* (1959), *Kent and the Civil War* (1960), *Some Aspects of Agriculture and Industry* (1961), *The Poor* (1964), *Some Kentish Houses* (1965) and *Crime and Punishment* (1969); and Essex County Council published *English History from Essex Sources, 1550–1900* (1952, 2 vols., out of print). All provide helpful evidence of what may be found in local archives elsewhere.

A good deal of inspiration can be gained from reading a few of the best local histories, such as those listed in the *English Local History Handlist*, e.g. for towns, those of Lincoln, Hitchin or Exeter, or for villages, those of Crawley (Hampshire), Hooton Pagnell (Yorkshire), King's Langley (Hertfordshire), or Deddington (Oxfordshire). *Local Studies: Bishop Auckland* (H.M.S.O., 1948) illustrates work in a Secondary Modern school; *The Story of Upminster* (12 pamphlets, 1957–60) was produced by the Upminster Local History Group inexpensively and proved to be a best-seller; *Chichester Papers* (obtainable from Messrs. Phillimore) include many pamphlets; and *Wheatley Records* (Oxfordshire Record Society, 1953) show the alternative of presenting extracts from archives instead of tackling a complete narrative village history. R. B. Pugh's *How to Write a Parish History* (1954) is not everyone's ambition and sets a very high standard, whereas W. G. Hoskins's *Local History in England* is more encouraging to the beginner and emphasizes the need for fieldwork: 'Some of the best documented local histories betray not the slightest sign that the author has looked over the hedges of his chosen place, or walked its boundaries, or explored its streets, or noticed its buildings and what they mean in terms of the history he is trying to write.'

For those engaged in biographical studies or their own family history, Hamilton-Edwards, *In Search of Ancestry*, and A. J. Willis, *Genealogy for Beginners* are among several recent books; and *Genealogists' Magazine* (Phillimore for the Soc. of Genealogists) is also useful.

This section may fittingly end with reference to the monumental work of S. and B. Webb dealing with the history of *English Local Government* from 1689 onwards, especially the volumes on *The Parish and the County*, *The Manor and the Borough*, *English Poor Law History*, *The Story of the King's Highway*, and *Statutory Authorities for Special Purposes*.

Students should not overlook the vast amount of local material in the long series of Public Record Office *Calendars* and *Lists and Indexes* and Historical Manuscripts Commission *Reports*.

II

Local Repositories

(*Note.* The reader wishing to have brief particulars of nearly all the national and local archive institutions including the larger libraries should consult *Record Repositories in Great Britain* (H.M.S.O., for Historical Manuscripts Commission, 1964), arranged under London and counties, Wales, etc.)

Long before the establishment of the first county and city record offices in the 1920s most public libraries and a few museums had acquired some historical documents relating to their town and the surrounding area. They were the places to which such documents tended to gravitate in the absence of local archive repositories. From a much earlier period the British Museum and the great university libraries at Oxford and Cambridge, whilst acquiring collections, had absorbed large numbers of documents mainly of local interest. Certain old-established institutions such as the John Rylands Library, Manchester, were doing the same.

Thus, during the last century and well into this century, the chief preservers of local MSS. were archaeological societies and town libraries, and students should never forget the debt owed to them. Some librarians and curators merely 'took them in' to safeguard them from destruction: with the upsurge of interest in local history many of these documents have come to light again, after being stowed away and almost forgotten. A few public libraries, however, for many years followed an active policy of searching for local documents. In certain boroughs archives departments have been set up in their libraries or museums in recent years, and these have developed alongside the county record offices. A few university libraries also began to collect local manuscripts as part of a definite policy, or to enlarge earlier collections. Other repositories act jointly for two or more local authorities or similar bodies.

More particulars about all these types of institutions are given in the succeeding sections.

But, in the main, county record offices, starting with the great series of their own official records, to which have been added vast accumulations of semi-official and private archives received from other sources, now offer the widest scope for students of local archives. It seems logical, therefore, to deal first with them; then to describe the other official repositories such as borough record offices; and lastly to refer to the repositories with chiefly artificial 'holdings' (an American term now generally adopted) rather than official records, and these include some libraries and a few museums.

County Record Offices

Soon after the creation of county councils in 1889, a few, such as Middlesex, Worcestershire, Shropshire and Hertfordshire, had begun to take a practical interest in the ancient records of their predecessors, the Courts of Quarter Sessions, by engaging experts to repair the oldest sessions rolls and to prepare and print calendars (detailed abstracts).

The first county council to create a county record office with a permanent salaried staff of one archivist was that of Bedfordshire in the 1920s, and that developed into what was generally regarded as the model before the Second World War. Very slowly other county councils followed. Even by 1938 only a dozen county record offices had been established with full-time salaried staffs ranging from one to six members. The really rapid increase took place after the war. Now there is a county record office in every county (usually in the County or Shire Hall) except for the West Riding of Yorkshire, Rutland, and a few Welsh counties for which the National Library of Wales acts. The West Riding of Yorkshire County Council contributes to the cost of the archive departments of the Leeds and Sheffield City Libraries, which provide a full service for the north and south parts of the Riding; the official County Records may be consulted at the County Hall, Wakefield.

Staffs range from two to twenty, comprising professional, technical, clerical and manual grades. A few county archivists are independent chief officers, but in most counties are under the control of the Clerk of the County Council, who was until 1972 also Clerk of the Peace and the statutory custodian of the Quarter Sessions records. The term county record office in many instances conceals wider functions, though a few make this clear by their specific title, e.g. 'Devon Record

Office and Exeter Diocesan Record Office', or by their notepaper, e.g. 'Lincolnshire Archives Committee for the Diocese and County of Lincoln (incorporating the Lincoln Diocesan Record Office)' and 'Essex Record Office, incorporating County Record Office (Quarter Sessions and Lieutenancy Records), Diocesan Record Office (Wills, Archdeaconry and Parish Records), Manorial Repository (Estate and Family Archives and Maps), Library (Essex books, prints, photographs and pictures)'.

Fuller information about the groups and classes of records and the like is given in the next chapter. Here we are concerned rather in trying to give in a general way some idea of the main groups which may or may not be housed in county, borough and other local record offices and libraries. This is perhaps best explained by taking one by one the various capacities in which a county record office may act.

Diocesan Record Offices

A few dioceses have their own archivist (the University provides Durham's). Nearly thirty English county record offices have been formally recognized by the Anglican bishops as diocesan record offices. The National Library of Wales serves for the whole Province of Wales. All these hold the ancient archives of bishops' and/or archdeacons' courts and other diocesan and archidiaconal records, including usually the registrars' copies of the parish tithe awards and maps and (if surviving) the transcripts of parish registers sent annually to the bishop or archdeacon. The Parochial Registers and Records Measure (Church Assembly), 1929, also provided for the establishment of diocesan record offices for the reception of parish records.

Probate Repositories

Nearly thirty local repositories now hold almost all the pre-1858 wills proved in the former local ecclesiastical courts, but they do not quite coincide with the 'nearly thirty' English diocesan record offices referred to in the previous section.

Manorial Repositories

During the past forty years nearly all county record offices, most of the borough libraries with archives departments and a few other places have been officially approved by the Master of the Rolls for the deposit of manorial documents. As manorial documents usually form part of the much larger archive group of Estate and Family Archives, such repositories also house the latter.

Borough Record Offices

Some of the very important municipal corporations and a few of the small but very ancient corporations have established record offices with full-time city or borough archivists (most of whom have one or more assistants) on the staff of the Town Clerk, who is the legal custodian of the corporation records. The Corporations of London (see p. 16) and Bristol, very appropriately, were among the pioneers in this respect. The official records of the older and more populous boroughs are even more diverse in character than those of the bigger counties. Some city and borough record offices accept few or no unofficial records, but others, like all county record offices, are active in inviting the deposit of estate, business and family archives.

Borough Libraries and Museums

In the course of the past fifty or one hundred years a library may have received several hundred gifts and deposits of ancient local documents. Each may range from a single manuscript to a great collection, especially where the library had gained later the status of a manorial repository. Whereas borough record offices contain relatively few documents which do not concern the borough, it is important to note that borough libraries have usually collected material not only for the town but also for a wider surrounding area. In the days before county record offices were set up, some libraries, especially those in county towns, actively sought historical manuscripts for the whole county. Between the two World Wars, indeed, the City Librarian of Exeter (there being then no county record offices for Devon and Cornwall) secured many documents for both counties. Between forty and fifty city and borough libraries have fairly large collections of manuscripts, and about one-fourth of this number now have separate departments in charge of archivists. The majority of the Greater London borough libraries likewise have historical manuscripts and some have archivists.

A few corporations, on the Town Clerk's recommendation or with his concurrence, have also placed their older official records in the city or borough library, which then virtually has the status of a borough record office. Exceptionally, at Leicester, Guildford and Hastings, the Corporation museum, not the library, acts as an archive repository.

Joint Repositories

Soon after the Second World War, a number of neighbouring local authorities decided to combine in setting up local record offices. As such joint repositories are confusing to the student, the more important of these are given:

Cumberland, Westmorland and Carlisle R.O. (The Castle, Carlisle, and County Hall, Kendal).
Lincolnshire Archives Office, acting for all three County Councils and City of Lincoln (The Castle, Lincoln).
Norfolk and Norwich R.O. (Central Library, Norwich).
Bury St Edmunds and West Suffolk R.O. (8 Angel Hill, Bury).
Ipswich and East Suffolk R.O. (County Hall, Ipswich).
Monmouthshire and Newport R.O. (County Hall, Newport).

In addition, the Staffordshire R.O. (County Buildings, Stafford) is linked with the William Salt Library, Stafford, and the Lichfield Diocesan R.O. (Bird St., Lichfield); the Wiltshire R.O. (County Hall, Trowbridge) administers the Salisbury Diocesan R.O. (56c The Close, Salisbury); and the Lincolnshire Archives Office includes the Diocesan R.O. for the former vast diocese.

Other Local Repositories

Thus the pattern of local record offices, unlike the archive offices for each department in France, was not created, but evolved in a typically English, haphazard manner, chiefly as a result of one or two persons' enthusiasm for their county or town. Local inhabitants, especially those of the smaller towns, may justly take pride in having established an archive repository at an early date which gained its independence or maintained its semi-independence in joint working arrangements with the county council.

But the brief account so far given by no means refers to all the repositories housing local archives. Some were established long before local record offices were envisaged. As a brief guide to the reader, the following list, admittedly incomplete, may prove helpful. It gives the larger local repositories which do not fall into any of the preceding categories, and is arranged by counties:

Chief Local Repositories other than County and Borough Record Offices and Public Libraries and Museums with Archives Depts:

BUCKINGHAM County Museum, Aylesbury (Bucks. Arch. Soc.).

CAMBRIDGE University Library (holds many Cambs. and East Anglian MSS., also acts at Ely Diocesan R.O.).

DURHAM The Prior's Kitchen, The College, University of Durham (holds the records of the Dean and Chapter, the Palatinate and Bishopric, Consistory Court probate records, and estate MSS.).

HEREFORD Cathedral Library (holds the records of the Dean and Chapter).

KENT Cathedral Library and Archives and City Record Office, The Precincts, Canterbury (also acts as Diocesan Record Office for Canterbury).

LANCASTER John Rylands and Chetham's Libraries, both Manchester (hold many Lancs. and Cheshire MSS.).

LONDON (See below.)

NOTTINGHAM Nottingham University, Dept. of Manuscripts (acts as a Manorial and Tithe Documents Repository).

OXFORD Bodleian Library (holds large collections of English local MSS., also acts as Manorial, Tithe Documents and Diocesan Record Office for Oxfordshire and Berkshire).

STAFFORD Keele University Library.

SUSSEX Barbican House, Lewes (Sussex Arch. Trust).

WARWICK Shakespeare's Birthplace Trust Library, Stratford-on-Avon (also holds borough records).

YORK Borthwick Institute of Historical Research, St Anthony's Hall, York (holds the archiepiscopal records of the Province, also acts as Diocesan Record Office).

YORKSHIRE Archaeological Society's Library, 10 Park Place, Leeds.

WALES

CAERNARVON University College Library, Bangor (acts as a Manorial and Tithe Documents Repository).

The National Library of Wales, Aberystwyth (also acts as a Manorial and Tithe Documents Repository and as Diocesan Record Office for Province of Wales).

Local Repositories in Greater London

CITY OF LONDON

Two archive repositories are maintained by the Corporation. The Records Office, Guildhall, is restricted to the official Corporation records. The Guildhall Library houses the majority of the parish and livery company archives and quantities of private and business archives.

COUNTY OF LONDON

Although the London County Council was created only in 1889 (it was superseded by the Greater London Council in 1965), it took over the functions of the bodies shown in the chart on p. 17. These, with the exception of Parish and Guardians records, are summarized in the *Guide to the Records in the London County Record Office*, Part I (1962); the repository is in the County Hall, Westminster Bridge. In addition, it is a diocesan, manorial and tithe record office: it has no Quarter Sessions records, but has the land tax lists (p. 29) for South London parishes.

MIDDLESEX

The Middlesex Record Office, 1 Queen Anne's Gate Buildings, Dartmouth St., S.W.1, which is a normal county, diocesan, manorial and tithe record office, will not be affected, for some years at any rate, as regards its site or facilities, by the abolition of the Middlesex County Council in 1965 (now called Greater London R.O. (Middlesex)).

GREATER LONDON BOROUGHS

Large and important collections of manuscripts are held by Westminster City Library and by some of the Borough Libraries, a few of which also house official borough records and manorial documents. (See *Record Repositories in Great Britain* (1964), pp. 10–13; to these libraries may be added those of boroughs now in Greater London.)

National Repositories with Local Archives

This short title is a very inadequate term for the sixty or more non-local institutions listed under 'London' in *Record Repositories in Great Britain*. The amateur, after examining archives in a local repository, may well desire to follow up certain lines of inquiry by visiting one of the national institutions to see, for example, some of the minute books and maps of an early 'local' railway company now in the custody of the archivist to the British Railways Board, wills not proved in local courts and now in Somerset House, and papers relating to Local Acts now in the House of Lords Record Office. (See Appendix, 'Short Guides to Records – Estate Acts of Parliament'.) In addition to official guides, Surrey Record Society's Volume 24, *Guide to Archives relating to Surrey in the Public Record Office* helps local historians to get some idea of the labyrinthine wealth of that repository, but there is no strictly parallel county key to the manuscripts in the British Museum.

Archives not in Public Repositories

Parish records are being deposited in local record offices at a rapid rate, but many students will need to consult those still remaining in the hands of the clergy. A tactful approach by letter offering at least two alternative dates or times for the visit will usually secure reasonable facilities for examination. Estate and family archives in private custody can of course only be consulted if the owner is willing to give permission and if granted should be treated as a favour and every effort made to cause no inconvenience to the owner. His documents must be handled with scrupulous care. Similar remarks apply to old-established colleges, societies and banks. If in doubt, ask the Registrar, National Register of Archives, Quality Court, Chancery Lane, WC2.

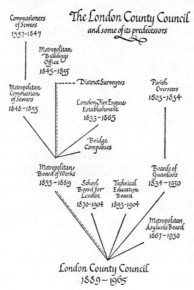

Reproduced from *Guide to the Records in the London County Record Office* Part I. 1962.

III

Visiting A Local Repository

Preparatory

One's first insight into local archives may be casual, through visiting an exhibition, for instance, but is more likely to arise from a definite aim. More and more people living in old houses, whether they possess ancient title-deeds or not, wish to discover whether original records tell something about its past. Local historical societies' lectures and excursions stimulate their members to find out for themselves something about their own town or village. And a still greater number of students at universities and colleges of education find that they are expected to do research on their own account, often including the examination of actual archives. Schoolteachers and senior children are also tackling manuscripts with zest and obtaining useful results. The rewards may depend largely upon the preliminary preparation. We shall see how this initial work may be effectively conducted.

Before visiting a local archives repository, whether a record office or the archives department of a large municipal library, the reader's first step is to find out if there is a printed *Guide* or other handlist of its chief contents. This should be on the shelves of his nearest public library. The number of such *Guides* is growing steadily. At present they are in print for the county record offices of Bedfordshire, Berkshire, Caernarvonshire, Essex, Flintshire, Gloucestershire, Hertfordshire, Huntingdonshire, Kent, Lancashire, Lincolnshire (*Handlist of Lincoln Diocesan Records*, also series of detailed *Annual Reports*), London, Middlesex, Monmouthshire, Nottinghamshire, Oxfordshire, Shropshire, Somerset, Staffordshire, West and East Sussex, Wiltshire, and Yorkshire (East Riding). All have been published by the county councils. Some are brief, and prices range from 25p to £1·50. The *Guide* for Northumberland, among other counties, is still in the press. For the city of London there is a combined *Guide* to the Corporation records and the Guildhall Library manuscripts. By now most cities and boroughs with archive departments in their town halls, libraries or museums have issued some form of handlist or catalogue; those for Birmingham, Sheffield, Leicester, Nottingham, Gloucester, Cardiff, Kingston-upon-Thames, and Southampton are among the best; Rye, Winchelsea and Seaford by East Sussex County Council. Some county councils have published, in advance of or in addition to a complete handlist, a *Catalogue* of a section of the archives, e.g. parish records (see p. 50), estate or county maps (p. 62). If the student does not find what he seeks in such publications, he should remember that great numbers of additional documents are received each year, brief details of which are given in the *List of Accessions to Repositories* published by H.M.S.O. for the National Register of Archives.

For some counties there are *Calendars* (detailed abstracts) of certain records, especially Quarter Sessions records, which may have run into many volumes (see p. 23), and the student owes a great debt to those county historical societies and county councils which have borne the cost of publication.

Articles about certain classes of records and certainly about selected documents will already be in print in the *Transactions* or *Publications* of the local historical, archaeological or record societies. The reader may have to consult the index to each volume, but if he is lucky he may find a *General Index* to many of the volumes already published. It is assumed that the student will also have looked at suitable books among those listed on pp. 7–9 before his first visit to a local repository to look at original sources. He is strongly advised to make an appointment by letter or telephone.

The request for an initial appointment should be brief but precise. A typical inquiry, for instance, from a trainee teacher, should include the name of his college, his subject (history, geography, etc.), his intended theme, and, if appropriate, a statement that he has already consulted some of the printed reference books in college or public library, including the Local Record Office *Guide* (or similar publication), from which he has noted the existence of A.B. papers (quoting page of the *Guide* may prove useful). His letter may finish with an inquiry as to whether there is other suitable material, and he should give two dates for his intended visit. The last point is strongly recommended because seating accommodation may be limited, and it will allow the archivist to state on which of the dates he may be relatively free to give the student a little preliminary guidance on the suggested topic. In reply the student may receive (or be given on arrival) a short printed or duplicated explanatory leaflet about the repository, its regulations and so forth, and he is advised to read it carefully. It may provide hints as to how to find the most useful reference works, catalogues and indexes on the shelves.

Above all, he should not be overbearing in his requests. To the archivist, any student's inquiry is one more call for assistance, and courtesy on the part of the student will evoke similar treatment.

It may be useful to give some indication of the help which the student may expect to receive. The archivist or assistant in charge of the search-room will normally answer, or show the inquirer how to find the answer to, such questions as: 'In which parish is the hamlet of A.B.?', 'In what year was C.D. sheriff?', 'Was the parish of F a peculiar (exempt from the jurisdiction of bishop or archdeacon)?', 'Is Willett the correct reading of this faintly written surname?', and 'Will you please translate this short Latin phrase?' If the record office has a good reference library and an explanatory leaflet about the 'means of reference', then the student may be expected to discover the answers for himself as part of his research experience. A local ratepayer, however, paying one or two visits only for a specific purpose may reasonably expect to get a little more help.

A question such as: 'Is class X.Y. likely to yield information on my subject or not?' is a fair one if the catalogue is only a bare summary, but not so if it is detailed or has a good introduction giving the information sought. 'Will you please help me – I am afraid I can't read more than a few words in this document' or 'I do not know where all these parishes are' is out of order and can only lead to an invitation to buy or borrow and study a book on handwritings or the local Ordnance Survey sheets and work it out for himself. Writing of his own students, Mr John West, formerly a senior training college lecturer with wide experience of local record offices, said: 'Often they antagonize the most patient archivist by demanding more help than they should expect; usually their inquiries are vague, and their intention over-ambitious' (*Village Records* (1962), p. 2). Since then, archivists have been gratified with the correct procedure now followed by the majority of trainee teachers.

Facilities: Hours, Reproductions, etc.

It is impossible to generalize briefly about the hours during which documents may be consulted in local repositories. Those in County and Borough Councils' offices are usually open to students from about 9.15 a.m. to 5.15 p.m., but few are open on Saturdays since a five-day week was introduced. Some with small staffs close for the lunch period. A few, such as the Essex Record Office, also open one evening a week. But hours are longer in those public libraries having archives departments and usually shorter in the 'other local repositories' listed on p. 15. Pens are banned in a few offices; typewriters, by special arrangements, are allowed in others. Notice of visits is asked for, in both parties' interests, but may be waived if the request is for readily accessible documents. Permission should be sought for tracing maps. The greatest care should be used at all times in handling documents, especially large maps, and in some repositories photographs of maps are produced in order to save wear and tear on the originals. For the use of parish registers, see p. 54.

Equipment for making photographs or the cheaper contact or reflex types of reproduction varies from office to office, though facilities are increasing gradually almost everywhere. Charges are usually moderate, but some repositories are obliged to ask students to make their own arrangements with commercial photographers. Microfilms of many types of documents, except those of large size such as most maps, can be supplied in some offices, and the majority now possess microfilm readers.

The public often offers fees for searches or transcripts of documents, but this is not a normal service of a national or local record office, and arrangements have to be made with a professional record agent in London or the provinces, although a few offices have domestic facilities.

IV

Using Local Archives

Introductory

'I had no idea that I might *discover* the old deeds of my house in the local record office – my Stuart and Tudor ancestors in this parish although the pre-1700 registers are lost – a map showing all the strips in the open fields in our parish before the enclosure – the eighteenth-century field-names of my farm – all the villagers' names in an old rate-book – court rolls of our manor going right back to Henry VIII – the wills of hundreds of the High Street tradesmen in Georgian times – scores of new references to clockmakers for my book on Blankshire clocks – the village school log-book of a century ago – a list of all the nonconformist chapels in the county in 1829 and many earlier applications for registration.' These and scores of similar grateful remarks are among archivists' rewards, though of course some visitors go away disappointed owing to a dearth of material for a given parish, family or subject, hoping perhaps that more may turn up later.

In this chapter the reader will be introduced to the main *groups* of local archives (e.g. county Quarter Sessions, diocesan, borough or estate archives) and to the *classes* (e.g. early registers of electors, wills, or maps) which are in most use by students.

An attempt will be made to describe briefly a few of the chief subjects on which each class may throw light. If you have no time to read through the following chapters, the index at the end may direct you to the class or classes you need to consult. Remember that, if the local repository has issued a *Guide* or other publications, it should be consulted for further details.

County Records – Quarter Sessions and Clerk of the Peace

The County Records proper, that is, those of the justices in Quarter Sessions and of their officer, the Clerk of the Peace, yield information on a wide range of subjects, e.g.

Crimes, offences and punishments, police, gaols and houses of correction, roads and bridges, poor relief and vagrancy, markets and fairs, weights and measures, rates of wages, inns and alehouses, agriculture, enclosure of open fields and commons, dissenters and Roman Catholics, charities, friendly societies and savings banks, canals, railways and other public schemes.

This heterogeneous list arises partly because the County Justices had both judicial and administrative functions, and secondly because a miscellaneous assortment of documents and lists of persons had to be enrolled, registered or deposited with the Clerk of the Peace for record purposes or for public inspection, which in due course have acquired historical interest.

The numerous Acts of Parliament which gave rise to some of these records, and the archives resulting from the justices' duties in and out of Quarter Sessions, are referred to in *County Records* (F. G. Emmison and Irvine Gray, Hist. Assoc., revd. edn., 1973) and more fully in the writer's *Guide to Essex Record Office*, Part 1 (revd. edn., 1969). The latter includes a classification scheme for Quarter Sessions records which has been adopted by most county archivists and may therefore prove useful to students when consulting typescript catalogues in those county record offices without a printed *Guide* (see p. 18). Both booklets print a number of copies or extracts from the records by way of examples.

The Quarter Sessions records for Cardiganshire, Montgomeryshire, and Radnorshire are now housed in the National Library of Wales, which also holds the records of the Courts of Great Sessions of Wales, 1542–1830.

THE COURT IN SESSION

For many counties the older *sessions rolls, minute-books* or *order-books* have been printed, in full or as more or less detailed calendars, by county councils or record societies. Unfortunately present-day printing costs have almost halted further publication. (The medieval Sessions records of a number of counties in the Public Record Office have nearly all been published.)

Here is a very brief summary of the counties and main periods for which Quarter Sessions rolls or books are in print:

Bedfordshire, 1651–60, extracts, 1714–1832; Buckinghamshire, 1678–1712; Caernarvonshire, 1541–58; Cheshire, extracts, 1558–1760; Derbyshire, extracts; Devonshire, extracts, chiefly sixteenth and seventeenth centuries; Dorsetshire, 1646–50; Hertfordshire,

1581–1894; Lancashire, 1590–1606; Lincolnshire (Kesteven), 1674–95; Middlesex, 1549–1618, 1689–1709; Norfolk, 1650–57; Northamptonshire, 1630, 1657–8; Nottinghamshire, extracts, seventeenth and eighteenth centuries; Oxfordshire, 1687–9; Shropshire, 1638–1889; Somersetshire, 1606–77; Staffordshire, 1581–1606; Surrey, 1659–66; Sussex, 1642–9; Warwickshire, 1625 96; Westmorland, extracts; Wiltshire, extracts, 1563–92 and seventeenth century; Worcestershire, 1591–1643; Yorkshire (W. Riding), 1598–1642; (N. Riding), 1605–1716, extracts, 1717–86.

In addition there are numerous unpublished calendars of Sessions rolls, e.g. for Essex, 1556–1714 (indexed). Most of the published volumes have a scholarly introduction explaining the nature of the court's judicial and administrative functions. Their contents are largely concerned with the crimes and offences which came before the J.P.s, and with roads, bridges, and the poor. (The most serious crimes were dealt with at Assizes; very few of the post-medieval Assize records, in the Public Record Office, have been published, but those for Essex, 1556–1714, have been calendared in typescript for the Essex Record Office.)

In most counties until recent years all the parchments and papers of one session were threaded on a single file. The main original documents for each session are *writs, indictments, recognisances* (various bonds for appearance at sessions, good behaviour and keeping the peace, etc.), *presentments, informations* (depositions) (Plate 11(a)), *jury panels, calendars of prisoners, petitions, accounts* for repair of bridges and gaols, *certificates* of various kinds. Such a file was then rolled up in a parchment cover and generally became known as a sessions roll. But in some of the more populous counties their bulk led to the papers such as petitions, presentments, informations or accounts being put in a separate roll, file or bundle for each session. Many specimen forms of writs, recognisances, indictments and presentments, mostly in Latin (untranslated) are printed in *Surrey Quarter Sessions Records*, vol. V (1934), pp. 88–122. Where the sessions rolls of a county have not been calendared or extracted in print or in typescript and still remain without any subject index or other finding aid, the student with little time to spare is advised not to examine them, as they are annoyingly difficult to handle, may be in need of repair, and usually include a fair proportion of documents in Latin or in somewhat illegible writing. In such circumstances he may find the *order-* or *minute-books* much easier to consult. Order-books are usually well written and some have brief contemporary indexes; while these relate chiefly to administrative matters, some judicial business may be included. (See Plates 6(b), 9(a), 11(b) and 17.) Many books may be drafts in less formal or legible writing, but may contain more entries of a judicial nature.

Highways, bridleways and footpaths, as well as county, hundred, parish and private bridges (Plate 11(b)), figure profusely, both in the judicial and the administrative documents, which may include plans and bills for building and repair. The justices built the county (or shire) hall (or sessions house), gaols and houses of correction, the police headquarters and stations, petty sessions court houses, and the lunatic asylum, for all of which there are usually many records.

Minor functions for which the county justices exercised control were rates of land carriage, assessments of wages of servants, labourers and artificers, weights and measures, and diseases of animals; they also had indirect duties in connection with the county militia, though this was mainly controlled by the Lord Lieutenant.

The extent to which the financial records of the county justices have survived varies from county to county and the total loss of early accounts in some counties results partly from the fact that the county treasurer was an honorary officer chosen from among the justices.

Of the many different kinds of documents registered or deposited with the Clerk of the Peace, some are of outstanding importance to the local historian. Some were filed on the sessions rolls, but from about 1700, especially in the larger counties, separate bundles, files or registers were usually started. The next five sections describe the chief classes.

PARLIAMENTARY ENCLOSURES

Enclosure awards are important records of commissioners appointed under individual Private and Local Acts or the General Inclosure Acts, 1836 and 1845 ('inclosure' is the spelling used by lawyers, 'enclosure' that adopted by historians). They relate to the enclosure and allotment of open fields and common meadows, or commons (Plate 31(a)), heaths, greens or forests, or land of both types, depending partly whether the parish lay within the open-field region.

The great majority belong to the period between about 1760 and 1860. Most have accompanying maps. Their value depends mainly according to the area dealt with in each award. At one end of the scale, the award may relate only to the village green or a few acres of heath or waste (many an urban place-name including 'heath' or 'green' refers to a pre-enclosure common); even where the common thus enclosed covered many acres the award and map may reveal only minor topographical detail. But awards dealing with the wholesale re-allotment of the open field strips into the new fields to be hedged are among the major records of the parish, especially if illustrated by a large-scale, accurately drawn map which usually covers the entire parish, including the village and the old closes. The field-names of the closes may also be given on the map, or occasionally in the award, with the owners' names. Many award maps show the boundaries and names of the former open fields.

If the land was enclosed at a late date (after 1830 or so), the enclosure commissioners' surveyor may have drawn a complete map of the strips in the open fields and meadows as a preliminary step towards putting the draft proposals for re-allotment to the landowners and commoners.

Such extremely interesting pre-enclosure ('strip') maps may also have been prepared by the tithe award surveyor (see pp. 41–42), if the tithes were apportioned at a date earlier than that of the enclosure; scores of other, and sometimes much earlier, strip maps have been found in private estate archives. (Plates 28(b), 29, 30.)

It is not generally known that many parliamentary enclosure acts authorized various other changes even beyond the far-sweeping re-allotment of the open fields, heaths and commons. In many parishes the tithes were completely extinguished by allotments of land to the parson (and to the lay rector, if the benefice was a vicarage), thus obviating the need for a later tithe award. Public roads, bridleways and footpaths, private occupation roads, public stone, gravel, chalk or marl quarries or pits, public drains, wells and watering-places, and (in late awards) even recreation grounds, were set out. In other respects, too, the award or the map may yield additional information of importance for local topography. Some awards are sufficiently detailed to enable a keen student who knows his parish well to reconstruct, accurately or approximately, the areas of the open fields and meadows, if the map itself does not indicate them.

Some enclosure awards and maps were not deposited with the Clerk of the Peace, but most county archivists have now succeeded in completing their series from other sources by acquiring originals or photographs. A duplicate copy may be in the Public Record Office or in the custody of the incumbent, clerk to the parish council or chief landowner. For many counties special lists of enclosure awards and maps were prepared (some of which have been printed) by the late W. E. Tate, who incorporated details of the parliamentary bills. The county archivist usually has information about the existence of such a list as well as of every known map and award. Printed catalogues of the enclosure awards and their maps have been compiled for several counties, e.g. Bedfordshire, Berkshire, Essex and Lancashire.

Enclosure awards before about 1825 were generally written by scribes who used somewhat archaic handwriting, but the student should not be put off, as a few minutes' reading will quickly familiarize him with the letters.

The minutes of the enclosure commissioners have been preserved for some parishes, and these throw light on the way in which claims for common rights and the like were settled.

The commons and open fields in some parishes were enclosed by private agreement between the lord of the manor and the tenants and those having rights of common. Such private enclosure records, some with maps, are still being discovered by local archivists, usually in estate archives of about 1700–1850, and the student should inquire where there is no public enclosure award. But he should know that there are very few awards for some counties such as Kent.

RELIGION

The Test Act of 1673 obliged everyone holding civil or military office to deliver to Quarter Sessions a certificate of his having received the Lord's Supper, signed by the minister, churchwardens and two witnesses. Many thousands of names are recorded in these *sacrament certificates* (Plates 13(a)) and later cognate documents. They became fewer after about 1750.

Registers of papists' estates, from 1716, give detailed descriptions of their properties.

Protestant dissenters' meeting-house certificates or applications for registration may have been preserved from the date of the Toleration Act of 1688; they cease in 1852. These give brief but valuable particulars of the owner or occupier of the property, and usually his denomination; they are often signed by several prominent dissenters (see p. 43).

DIVERSION AND CLOSURE OF ROADS

By an Act of 1773 a highway, bridleway or footway might be diverted or stopped up by two J.P.s provided that the new way was more convenient to the public. If there was no appeal, Quarter Sessions confirmed and enrolled the order and the accompanying map. Such maps were usually well drawn after about 1800, and some show details of parks. The owner tended to produce a plausible statement explaining how the public would benefit by a more convenient (but perhaps longer) route; that it might allow him to enlarge his park boundary beyond the closed road or might give him more privacy was not mentioned! (Plate 19.)

The printed *Calendars* of Quarter Sessions records for several counties, such as Bedfordshire and Hertfordshire, fully describe such roads and paths; the Hertfordshire *Guide*, vol. i, pages 88–112, also lists them alphabetically by parishes.

SCHEMES AND SOCIETIES

From 1792 onwards the promoters of Parliamentary Bills for public utility schemes had to deliver detailed plans to the Clerk of the Peace. They relate to river navigations and canals, harbours, docks and piers, waterworks and reservoirs, turnpike roads, railways and tramways, tunnels and large ferries, gas and electricity works, together with various other schemes such as drainage, reclamation of land, estuary and sea-front improvements. (Plate 32.) Many of the schemes, especially rival railway proposals, were abortive, and of course railway plans account for the great majority between 1835 and 1865.

The early manuscript plans are of great interest. The first railroad schemes related to horse-drawn tramways. In canal, road and railway schemes, fields and buildings within about a quarter of a mile on each side of the proposed course are recorded in both plans and the accompanying books of reference. Every county and borough record office has a detailed catalogue of these plans; a few have published the list, in their *Guides* or independently.

The annual accounts of turnpike trusts and gas and water companies from about 1829 onwards supplement the information obtainable from other sources.

Of interest also are the statutory returns, prescribed as public safeguards, relating to local charities, friendly societies, savings banks and printing presses. These consist largely of statements of the objects, officers and annual accounts, and they are mainly between about 1790 and 1870.

LISTS AND REGISTERS

Among the heterogeneous documents which the Clerk of the Peace had to file, copy or register were numerous lists of persons, of varying degrees of interest to the student. The Acts stating the reasons for publicly recording these names are quoted in most *Guides* to county record offices.

Among the earliest are *hearth tax assessments* between 1662 and 1688. These very valuable lists of householders in every parish give the number of hearths in each house, but some lists exclude poor persons. Only the county record offices of Caernarvonshire, Devonshire, Essex, Kent, Lancashire, Middlesex, Warwickshire and Westmorland hold them, and the majority are in the form of 'Exchequer duplicates' in the Public Record Office. Assessments for the following counties and towns have been printed, mostly in full and with scholarly introductions, viz. Bedfordshire, Cambridgeshire, Cheshire, Dorset, Oxfordshire, Shropshire, Somersetshire, Staffordshire, Suffolk, Surrey and Warwickshire; some include analyses dealing with the social and economic aspects of these important records. Unfortunately, however, names of houses and occupations are very rarely given. (See Appendix, 'Short Guides to Records – Hearth Tax Returns'.)

For almost every county much bulkier series of *land tax assessments*, one for every parish or township each year, are preserved, usually from late or mid-eighteenth century, even earlier for several counties but only from about 1800 in others. They were transmitted as evidence of one basis of a claim for a vote at parliamentary elections, and were superseded in 1832 by registers of electors. These lists give for each property the owner but not his abode or occupation; the occupier, if different (from 1786); the sum payable; and the rental, but this bears little or no relation to the actual rent as it was based on the original county assessments of 1692. In 1798 redemption of the tax became permissible; although the names of those who had commuted were sometimes given in subsequent lists, they gradually become less complete in this and other respects. From 1826 to 1832, however, there is an additional column for brief description of the property, e.g. land (or, more specifically, name of farm or inn, windmill, etc.); mills may be distinguished from a much earlier date. The value of land tax assessments for the effects of the parliamentary enclosure movement and on the survival of the small owners, though useful, has recently been qualified by Dr G. E. Mingay.[1]

The names of men between twenty-one and seventy in each parish qualified to serve on juries are recorded in *freeholders* (or *jurors*) *lists*, which have survived in some counties from 1696 but in others from a very much later date, and may be either original lists or copies in thin registers. Men are listed in their home parish, but that in which the

[1] 'The Land Tax Assessments and the Small Landowner' (*Econ. Hist. Rev.*, 2nd series, xvii, 381–8).

qualifying estate lies, if different, may be given, also age, annual value of property, and sometimes rank or occupation. An average parish list gives about four names – of gentlemen and the more substantial farmers, innholders and the like.

Registers of electors (1832 onwards) have been preserved in fairly complete series. The Act of 1832 widened the county franchise, previously limited to men with freehold worth at least 40s. a year, to include copyholders of £10, leaseholders of £50, and long leaseholders of £10 a year. Extensions of the franchise by the Reform Acts of 1867 and 1884 are reflected in immediate increases in the number of names. The entry for each voter gives his abode (the larger houses are named, and in the later registers the street and number); nature of qualifications, e.g. 'freehold mill', 'copyhold house'; and situation of qualifying property in the parish, hamlet or street, or its name (farm, inn, etc.).

Votes at elections are recorded in *poll-books*, which may exist for various dates from the latter half of the seventeenth century onwards, some in manuscript, others as contemporary printed versions. They may be bare lists of names set out under the parish in which the qualifying property lay, but the elector's abode (parish), if different, may be given; and some of the later books also give occupations. A few are in alphabetical order of electors. This brief note covers all poll-books, not merely those in the County Records. Most public libraries have a good local collection. (See Appendix, 'Short Guides to Records – Poll Books'.)

Gamekeepers registers, 1711–1889, are valuable because they also record the name of the manor and the lord at the date when he 'deputed' the power of killing game to his keeper.

The annual *licensed victuallers registers*, 1753–1828, preserved for most counties, give the inns and alehouses and publicans' names in each parish with their signs. They are a useful factual source for the history of inns, but give no other details, and the frequency with which names of inns changed should be borne in mind. (In some counties much earlier licensed victuallers' bonds for good behaviour are also extant, but seldom give the signs.)

Few of the published *Calendars* of County Records touch upon the wealth of information in these various registers and other documents deposited with the Clerk of the Peace. The Hertfordshire series, volumes vi–x, is a notable exception, listing all the names of lords of manors and gamekeepers, dissenters and roman catholics and sacrament certificate holders; Surrey, volume v, gives all the lords of manors, 1789–1860; and Warwickshire, volume viii, all nonconformist meeting-houses, 1660–1750.

Petty Sessions Records

Courts of Quarter Sessions were empowered in 1828 to create within each county districts or divisions for Petty Sessions, thus regularizing earlier informal divisions. The gradual and sporadic appearance of Petty and Special Sessions is outside our scope; in a few counties, notably Essex in the sixteenth century, they occur as hundredal sessions for the hiring of labourers; in others, as special, privy, or monthly sessions; all differing in origin and purpose. Formal minute-books of some Petty Sessions are extant for the eighteenth century, notably Kent (Plate 9(b)), and occasionally the relevant papers from about 1800. Most of the later minute-books have recently been transferred to county and borough record offices.

Shrievalty Records

In contrast to the immense quantity of ancient records of the Justices of the Peace and the Clerk of the Peace, few records of the Sheriff exist among the official county records. Students such as trainee teachers are therefore advised not to plan research projects on these officers' activities unless the *Guide* to their local record office reveals more than the usual amount of material.

Chance survival of the papers of an individual sheriff in family archives may however afford an interesting subject for study. The delightful 'Expenses extraordinary on account of ye Sheriffwick' of a Hertfordshire sheriff in 1717, printed in R. L. Hine, *Relics of an Uncommon Attorney*, (1951), pp. 14–16 (now in the Herts. R.O.), illustrate the duties in connection with the Assizes and prisoners. Every county record office has more than one example of a sheriff's 'quietus', the annual receipt-roll of the Exchequer for the Crown dues and fines at Quarter Sessions accounted for by him. He was also responsible for elections of knights of the shire and for juries at Assizes and Quarter Sessions. (Plate 1(a).)

Except for those of recent date, not open to students, Coroners' records in local record offices are so rare that nothing need be said about them.

Lieutenancy Records

An act of 1662 made the Tudor office of Lieutenant of the County permanent, and gave him in place of the Sheriff complete control over the County Militia. (Plates 1 and 3.) This was reorganized by an Act of 1757, from which date or slightly later minute-books of the Clerk to the Lieutenancy exist in some counties. By far the most important Lieutenancy records are those of the French Revolutionary and Napoleonic Wars, and preparations against invasion resulted in detailed minute-books and called for detailed returns in 1797 and 1803. For some counties incomplete statements from many parishes survive. These give the names of men fit to act as troops, guides or pioneers, and 'the implements they can bring' (with columns for 'felling axes', 'pick axes', spades, shovels, bill hooks, saws); the number of carts available; and millers' returns state the condition of windmill or watermill and the number of sacks of flour which they could produce daily, while bakers' returns give the number of loaves they could supply, if the emergency should arise. For some counties, too, militia muster rolls exist for various periods after 1803; these may give a thousand or more names. The Essex and Sussex *Guides* give fairly full details of Lieutenancy records.

Records of Statutory Authorities for Special Purposes[1]

COMMISSIONERS OF SEWERS

The maintenance of walls and embankments against the inroads of the sea and tidal rivers was entrusted to local bodies known as Commissioners of Sewers, whose rate-books, orders, minutes, presentments, accounts, surveys, maps and other records have mostly been transferred in recent years to the appropriate county record offices. They may date from the sixteenth to the beginning of this century. A wealth of topographical detail may be drawn from them relating to sea and river walls, marshes, roads, sluices and mills on tidal rivers in areas liable to sea-flooding; the surveys and maps may give many field-names. The Fens were a special problem. (Plate 24(a).) The rate-books deal only with the marshy lands in parishes affected, but for such areas the owners and occupiers assessed are set out in much the same form as poor rate-

[1] S. & B. Webb, *Statutory Authorities for Special Purposes* (1922) is very useful in connection with the history and records of the bodies dealt with in this chapter and of several other authorities.

lists. The *Court Minutes of the Surrey and Kent Sewer Commissioners,* 1569–79, the original records of which are in English and are now in the Greater London Record Office, were printed in full by the London County Council (1909).

TURNPIKE TRUSTS

The inability of a small or poor parish to maintain a stretch of a main highway which ran through it and the general deterioration of the more important thoroughfares gradually convinced the nation that the Act of 1555 served only for the upkeep of the country roads and lanes and that the users of the highways joining the larger towns ought to pay toll for their repair. Beginning in 1663 with a stretch of the Old North Road (not the Great North Road, as so often stated) in Cambridgeshire and part of the London–Harwich road in Essex in 1695, over 400 Turnpike Acts had appeared on the Statute Books by the mid-1700s, but progress was very slow in the more remote parts of the country. Turnpike roads were essentially local in origin, the sponsors being mainly groups of J.P.s and other landowners. Construction of maps for each county, or for smaller areas, would show that even the main thoroughfares were improved only in intermittent lengths, and such maps should prove to be instructive. (Extracts, 20, p. 99.)

The history of the chief highways and of most roads between market towns from about 1700 and 1875 is therefore to be sought in the minutes, accounts, maps and other archives of the turnpike trusts. As with Highway Board records, they reveal how the slipshod 'pecking of ruts' and so forth by parish surveyors was replaced by the superior maintenance and improvement schemes undertaken by the trusts' surveyors and engineers. Many of these were trained and a few, like Telford, Metcalfe and Macadam, experimented with new techniques.

BOARDS OF GUARDIANS

Although Gilbert's Act, 1782, authorized parishes to combine for setting up a 'proper' workhouse (p. 59), the vast majority of parishes continued to cope independently with the alarming problem and appalling burden of poor relief – an archaic and outmoded system for which the laissez-faire attitude of the government is almost incomprehensible to ourselves. When, at last, parishes were compulsorily grouped into Poor Law Unions by the Act of 1834 and the administration devolved upon elected Guardians of the Poor, the union areas were centred upon

D

the larger market towns, and where towns lay near county boundaries parishes in two or more counties were placed together under the new *ad hoc* authority. (Extracts, 21.)

Legislation demanded the keeping of a variety of registers by the Guardians and the masters of the Union workhouses. The bulk of these statutory records created by the more populous unions became enormous, and despite destruction and losses great quantities came to county and borough record offices soon after 1930, when the Guardians' duties passed to County and County Borough Councils. The minute books are the most interesting records of the Guardians' work; they are usually complete from 1834 to 1930, and are easy to consult and some also have contemporary indexes. Any student about to tackle a mass of miscellaneous Guardians' records should first consult the introduction to *Sussex Poor Law Records* (West Sussex Record Office, 1960). (See Appendix, 'Short Guides to Records – Guardians' Minute Books'.)

LOCAL BOARDS OF HEALTH

These were established in many towns not being boroughs under an Act of 1848 and were superseded by Urban District Councils in 1894. Their minutes, accounts and other records provide invaluable evidence of the grave lack of sanitation in the mid-1850s and of the rudimentary attempts to combat epidemics and disease. (Extracts, 22, 23 and p. 56.)

HIGHWAY BOARDS

In 1862 Quarter Sessions were empowered to set up Highway Districts by the compulsory combination of parishes. They were abolished between 1894 and 1900, and their powers were transferred to County Councils.

Their minutes and accounts of course reveal more efficient methods of road maintenance than those found in parish surveyors' records. For a few boards the letter-books and some working papers are also extant. (Extracts, 24.)

SCHOOL MANAGERS AND BOARDS

The earlier endowed schools will be referred to later (p. 50). The efforts of the British and Foreign School Society and the National Society for promoting the Education of the Poor created respectively many British Schools and National Schools, whose work was recognized by grants from the State, which in turn created the School Boards under Forster's Act of 1870. County Councils and County Borough Councils have taken over most of the early school plans, log-books (Extracts, 25, p. 104) and School Board minute-books, and those of older date are mostly open to students.

Borough Records

Professor F. J. C. Hearnshaw wrote in his pamphlet *Municipal Records* (S.P.C.K. Helps for Students, 1923): 'Not only are they so numerous as almost to defy examination, they are also so various as wholly to baffle classification. The most unexpected discoveries reward the curiosity of the patient explorer. The main varieties of records in the true meaning of the expression are: (1) Charters; (2) Accounts of Stewards, Chamberlains and other officials; (3) Guild Rolls and Ordinances; (4) Court Rolls; (5) Assembly Books; (6) Books of Examinations and Depositions; (7) Books of Miscellaneous Memoranda.' Even so, he omits big classes such as Deeds and (in some towns) Correspondence.

While no official County Records antedate the 1530s, some of the ancient corporate towns possess muniments of the twelfth century and even earlier. Pride of place is usually given to the series of borough charters (Plate 8(b)), but there are equally important, interesting and informative classes such as the hundreds (or thousands) of old deeds of properties, of immense value for the topographical history of the town, and judicial, administrative and financial archives for almost every other aspect. (Plates 10 and 14.)

The larger and more ancient boroughs each had several courts with differing judicial and administrative functions. Court of Record, Court of Assembly, Mayor's Court, Sheriff's Court, Court of Sessions of the Peace and Gaol Delivery, Court of Requests, Pie-powder Court, Fair and Market Court, Staple Court, and Petty View are among the names met with in the records (and the courts in some cities had their own names, such as the Tolzey Court of Bristol). The proceedings, minutes or orders of two or more of these courts may be found entered at opposite ends or different sections of a volume; courts may have merged; or their names may have changed. Or, in smaller towns, the court may have merely been termed the Borough Court.

Manorial courts (p. 65) also figure among borough archives. Those of Guildford include sixteenth-century books catalogued as 'Three-weekly Courts of the Lord, the annual Legal Court of View of Frank-pledge, and three Gilds Merchant' (Plate 15(a)), and eighteenth-century books contain General Quarter Sessions and Courts of the Clerk to the Market, or Wardmote Courts and Courts of the Clerk to the Market. Some manors had the status of seigneurial boroughs, conferred by grant of the lord and not by royal charter. Generally, their records do not differ in form from those of other manors or in content from those of manors with urban characteristics. The student using borough records will thus not be surprised at finding other peculiarities in names, classes and contents. Some boroughs have old Coroners' records.

The records of Borough Sessions and the Clerk of the Peace are similar to those of County Quarter Sessions and their Clerk (see pp. 22–30); and Borough records (especially County Borough records) of later date usually include those of Guardians of the Poor, Turnpike Trusts, Charity Trusts, Boards of Health, School Boards, and so forth (pp. 33–35). In many boroughs will also be found records of other *ad hoc* bodies such as Commissioners for Paving, Lighting and Watching. For the modern period there may be voluminous archives of the water and other utility undertakings. Maritime boroughs in addition possess records of the port, harbour and quays, varying in quantity and import-ance with the antiquity and trade of the port; these may include Admiralty Court books.

The archives of some eighty ancient boroughs were described and in some cases listed in detail in the older Reports of the Historical Manuscripts Commission, complete sets of which are in some borough libraries. The publications of some local archaeological, historical and record societies include important catalogues of borough archives. County archivists are becoming more and more involved with borough records, especially those of the smaller boroughs without an archivist, and their records are now being deposited in increasing numbers in county record offices, e.g. Berkshire, Sussex and Kent; the last has also been entrusted with the important Cinque Port archives.

This is a very inadequate and incomplete sketch, and the student who cannot find a printed catalogue of the records of the borough in which he is interested is advised, before examining them, to familiarize himself in general by looking at printed accounts of the records of other boroughs, e.g. those on p. 19. But catalogues are necessarily precise, and the student should then allow his enthusiasm to be revived by reading one or two of the best town histories, such as those of Lincoln,

Exeter, Hitchin, or Wednesbury. There are also several good histories dealing with relatively new towns or with social and economic development during the past century, especially stimulating to students of recent times. Suggested lines of inquiry on this important aspect of town growth in both medieval and modern periods are ably dealt with in W. G. Hoskins's *Local History in England* (1959).

Modern Local Authority Records

No general guidance can be given on the extent to which the modern records of County, Borough, Urban and Rural District Councils and other local authorities may be consulted, with special permission, by genuine students. Individual application, stating precisely the object, would in any case be necessary.

Ecclesiastical Records (excluding Wills and Parish Records)

(*The best book is Dorothy Owen's* Records of the Established Church (*British Records Association, 1970*). *For Probate and Parochial records, see* Wills and Inventories, *pp. 44–49, and* Parish Records, *pp. 50–61.*)

Unless the reader's interest in local archives is very specialized, he should not omit this chapter, thinking that Ecclesiastical Records relate solely to religion and churches: far from it, they throw light on a very wide variety of subjects.

The Church in medieval England, through its archbishops and bishops, cathedrals and parish churches, owned much property, especially land, which gave rise to great quantities of records. It controlled a hierarchy of courts, whose activities also gave rise to innumerable archives. And within the Church, but largely independent of episcopal control, were the religious houses. By the end of the Middle Ages the abbeys and priories owned about one-third of the land of England, with correspondingly numerous muniments (charters and title-deeds) and other archives.

At the Dissolution, despite waves of destruction, enormous masses of records came into the hands of the Crown or the lay purchasers or grantees. Tens of thousands of these documents have been preserved, and these are now in the National Repositories or with the later estate archives of the families through which ownership of the monastic properties subsequently passed – and in recent years have largely been rediscovered through the inquiries of the Historical Manuscripts

Commission, the National Register of Archives, the British Records Association and local archivists.

The Dissolution did not materially affect the routine archives of the archbishops, bishops, archdeacons, and deans and chapters – the great series of registers, rolls and papers of their numerous courts right down to their own manor courts. These judicial and administrative records continued to grow, in the same way as their title-deeds and estate archives multiplied.

Some ecclesiastical records are difficult to understand as well as to decipher, and the difficulties are increased because of the variety of jurisdictions. These involve both areas and control (provinces, dioceses, archdeaconries, peculiars and parishes). The Marc Fitch Fund has recently begun to sponsor the detailed listing of episcopal and capitular records.

Among the helpful county record office *Guides* with introductory notes on ecclesiastical records are those for (West) Sussex, Kent, Lancashire and Essex; see also *The Archives of the York Diocesan Registry*. As many inquiries about the archives of bishops' and archdeacons' courts are wrongly sent to cathedrals, it may be useful first to refer to Cathedral archives, which are quite different in origin and nature.

CATHEDRAL (CAPITULAR) RECORDS

The administration of a cathedral and its endowments was (and still is) under the control of the Dean and Chapter. The principal records are the chapter act books, accounts and the usual estate archives. The best descriptions of capitular records are those at Chichester (*Guide to the West and East Sussex Record Offices,* pp. 119–30 and Lincoln (*Lincs. Archives Committee Report for 1952–53,* pp. 37–69), which reveal how much miscellaneous material may be found in such archives. Where no printed handlist is available, the county archivist will inform inquirers whether he has charge of capitular records or they remain in the cathedral. A very brief summary of such a group is given in the 23rd *Report of the Royal Commission on Historical Manuscripts for 1946–59* (1961), p. 35:

The Dean and Chapter, Hereford

Deeds, etc., Hereford Cathedral, Gloucester Abbey, Ewenny Priory, St Ethelbert's Hospital in Hereford, St Katherine's Hospital in Ledbury, mostly Herefordshire, Gloucestershire, Worcestershire, Salop, Radnorshire, Glamorganshire, eleventh–nineteenth centuries. Court rolls, accounts, rentals and surveys, thirteenth–eighteenth centuries.

DIOCESAN AND ARCHIDIACONAL RECORDS

The most important of the medieval records are the bishops' registers. But after the Reformation their entries relate largely to ordinations and institutions of the clergy and consecrations of churches; and other administrative series record a variety of information concerning the benefices and the clergy; few of these post-medieval archives, however, have been published. For the episcopal estates there are documents, running into many thousands in the case of the older and richer dioceses, such as Canterbury, Durham, Ely, Lincoln and York, similar to those normally found in estate archives, e.g. title-deeds, leases and agreements, manorial documents, surveys and maps (pp. 62–65).

There is some overlapping between diocesan and archidiaconal records. Unlike bishops, archdeacons did not keep registers of ordinations and so forth, nor did they own estates. With these chief exceptions, the remaining classes of documents described in this section are found either in bishops' or archdeacons' archives (or in both), depending largely on their respective jurisdictions.

Some extensive dioceses, such as York and Lincoln, were divided into many archdeaconries, and those archdeaconries which were distant from the see, such as Richmond and Bedford (which coincided in area with the county), had a jurisdiction largely co-ordinate with, rather than subordinate to, the episcopal court.

But distance alone was not necessarily the factor which led to semi-independent status. For example, Essex, in the Diocese of London until 1846, lay in the archdeaconries of Essex, Colchester, and Middlesex ('Essex and Hertfordshire jurisdiction', which covered west and north Essex and part of east Hertfordshire originally in the Saxon kingdom of Essex); there were several 'peculiars' (mostly single parishes) exempt from the control of the bishop or archdeacons; and there were other concurrent jurisdictions, e.g. many parishes subject to the bishop's commissary for probate of wills but otherwise subject to the archdeacon! (The complications in Lancashire are mentioned on p. 45.)

The bishop's (or consistory) court for ecclesiastical causes and offences was held usually by his chancellor or commissary and the archdeacon's court by a commissary or 'official'. The judicial records of these courts, like those of quarter sessions, may be bulky, but their contents are not so readily accessible or intelligible to the ordinary student unless provided with some form of index, and few have been published. As the handwriting is often extremely difficult to read, and many of the Latin phrases are abbreviated, beginners are advised not to attempt to use the court act books (minutes) unless they are prepared to spend some time in mastering the form of the documents. The majority of the offences were concerned with breaches of discipline by clergy or laity, or were matrimonial, defamation or tithe cases, or related to probate of wills or administration of intestates' property. The best general aid, giving transcripts and explanatory notes, is J. S. Purvis, *Introduction to Ecclesiastical Records* (1953), St Anthony's Hall Publications, Borthwick Institute of Historical Research, York. Of help also are the same editor's *Tudor Parish Documents of Diocese of York* (1948), dealing with the interesting records of tithe suits in York consistory court archives, his *Dictionary of Ecclesiastical Terms* (1962), Miss K. Major, *Handlist of the Records of the Bishop of Lincoln* (1953), and chapter xix of L. Redstone and F. W. Steer, *Local Records* (1953).

Of greater interest to most students (and much easier to read, because they are largely or wholly in English) are the post-Reformation visitation books. These record under each parish presentments or returns concerning the condition (especially if defective) of the church fabric, furniture, ornaments, bells, plate, churchyard walls; delinquencies of clergy, church officers and parishioners, such as schoolmasters teaching without licence, trading or working on Sunday, playing football during service-time, drunkenness, and of course recusancy (absence from church). (Plate 4.) Bishop's visitations were held, in theory, every three years; those of archdeacons annually. (See Appendix, 'Short Guides to Records – Episcopal Visitation Books', which applies equally to those in archidiaconal archives.)

Some students may also be prepared to tackle the depositions in the cause (case) papers. Their form can be grasped after brief explanation, and they contain a mass of information of such varied topics as descriptions of parish boundaries, rural customs, farming practices, prices of commodities, and copies of earlier charters.

The diocesan (or archidiaconal) registrar preserved many routine documents about presentations to and resignations from benefices and about licences to incumbents for non-residence, to curates, parish clerks, and schoolmasters (Plate 5), also to surgeons and midwives who could then baptize in case of emergency. In addition the registrar received documents on deposit in much the same way as the Clerk of the Peace and some of these are very numerous.

Certain classes, now described, are much used by students because of their parochial, biographical or genealogical interest.

TITHE AWARDS AND MAPS

Among the most important diocesan records are the eight thousand Tithe Awards of about 1838–50, prepared for the majority of parishes, under the Tithe Act, 1836, when most tithes in kind were finally commuted by fixed rent-charges apportioned on each plot. A survey of the parish was made by a professional valuer, and the resultant records were an apportionment or award and a large-scale map. (Plate 31(b).) Occasionally, if a slightly earlier parish map had been made, that was adopted and copied.

Every field and dwelling is shown on the map and bears a number referring to the apportionment or schedule, which has columns for: owner; occupier; description, e.g. 'Hill Farm', 'George Inn', 'two cottages', 'Tainter Field', 'plantation' (details of the amount varies from parish to parish); use (arable, pasture, wood, or house, shop, etc.); exact acreage; sum payable. A similar extract (from a Worcestershire tithe map) is in *Village Records*, with the corresponding part of the apportionment. (Plates xiv, xc, and pp. 147–54.) The arrangement of entries in the apportionment is alphabetical by owners' names, so that most present-day users have to search through many parchment folios to find the entry for a given field or house. The preamble to the award may refer to land which is tithe-free or pays a modus or composition, usually of ancient origin, thus enabling the student to identify it perhaps with an estate of a former abbey or priory. Many of the maps show dwellings in red and other buildings in grey. The majority mark (and usually give the names of) commons, greens and heaths, but seldom give precise information about rights of way; some maps name the farms. A delightful feature often seen is a careful miniature drawing of a windmill, even distinguishing between post-mills and tower-mills. Many field-names, however, were unreliably recorded from local pronunciation! If the open fields and meadows were still unenclosed at the time of the tithe award, the map will show all the furlongs and strips. Other details depend on the locality: if a coastal parish, the map may clearly define harbours, quays and wharves, cliffs, marshes, marsh-drains, saltings and seawalls; if industrial, foundries, sheds, coalmines and the like; if urban, there may be invaluable detail, even an inset of the town area on a larger scale. Detached parts of parishes are carefully shown.

Three copies of each tithe award and map were prepared, for deposit with (1) the Tithe Commissioners, (2) the diocesan registrar, and (3) the incumbent. Of these, (1) may now be consulted at the Office of the

Tithe Redemption Commission, Finsbury Square, London, E.C.4, which has a complete set for the whole country; (2) is now normally in the county record office; (3) should still be in the parish (but many are lost or the maps have almost disintegrated as a result of frequent examination and careless storage), or it may be in the C.R.O.[1]

For some parishes there may also be one or many altered apportionments, each with a map. These relate to areas ranging from the whole parish to a few acres, the latter dealing with (say) amendments necessary after the building of a railway, the former following the rapid urbanization of a rural parish or growth of a town. Their chief interest is as evidence of building development and its date.

ANNUAL REGISTER TRANSCRIPTS

Under the Church injunction of 1597 each parish had to send an annual transcript of the entries in the register of baptisms, marriages and burials to the bishop (hence these were called 'Bishop's transcripts' even in those large dioceses for which the copies were sent to the archdeacon's registrar). Many thousands of these annual transcripts, usually on parchment and signed by the clergymen and churchwardens, have survived and are now mostly in county (diocesan) record offices, where they will generally be found arranged by parishes. In some areas they begin in 1598, elsewhere later or much later. Where extant, they are a most valuable substitute for missing or defective registers. Of the twenty thousand or so annual transcripts in the Archdeaconry archives in the Bedfordshire Record Office, which run from 1602 onwards, several thousands give the sole surviving baptisms, marriages and burials. The baptism of 'John the sonne of Thomas Bonnion Jun. the 30 of November', 1628, for example, comes from the transcripts for the parish of Elstow, the earliest register of which is lost. They also frequently help where entries in the original are illegible, and they occasionally give extra facts, such as occupation or mother's christian name, as well as different spelling for surname. The bishops' transcripts for Welsh parishes (mostly from about 1675) are in the National Library of Wales, Aberystwyth. (Plate 27.)

MARRIAGE LICENCES

Bonds and allegations preceding the issue of marriage licences form immense series of documents, especially where they have survived from

[1] An invaluable pamphlet on Tithe Records may be obtained gratis from the Commission's Office.

the earliest date (late sixteenth century). Licences were issued if both parties wished to marry outside their parish or without the banns being called. The facts given in marriage bonds and allegations are usually much fuller than those in parish registers. Details which may not be in the register are abode (parish), age (though after about 1785 parties may be given merely as 'over twenty-one' or 'minor' and if a minor parent(s) may be named), occupation (though often omitted), and two sureties, one of whom is usually a parent, relation or friend of the bridegroom. The bond begins: 'Know all Men by these Present that We (the two sureties) . . .'; and the allegation, starting with the date, 'On which day appeared personally (the groom) . . .' Series relating to some dioceses or archdeaconries have indexes compiled by genealogists, and some series have been published by local record societies. In such cases, the searcher, baffled by his inability to trace a desired marriage or disappointed by the omission of the parties' abodes or the man's occupation, may regard himself as fortunate. The documents are usually kept in big, annual bundles, so if no index exists and he has only a vague idea of the area or place, he will have to search in more than one bundle for more than one diocese or archdeaconry. Those for Wales are in the N.L.W., Aberystwyth.

GLEBE TERRIERS

Terriers, or surveys, exist for most parishes for certain episcopal visitation years from about 1600 onwards. These describe the rectory or vicarage house as well as the glebe land. The latter may consist of many strips in the open fields, and thus afford a partial picture of the fields and furlongs. Tithing customs and other items of agricultural interest are incidentally recorded. Some terriers also list the church plate, bells and books. (See Appendix, 'Short Guides to Records'.)

MEETING-HOUSE CERTIFICATES

Petitions, applications or certificates for registration of dissenters' chapels had to be sent *either* to the diocesan (or archidiaconal) registrar or to the Clerk of the Peace (p. 27).

FACULTIES AND CONSECRATIONS

Petitions for the issue of faculties and consecration deeds are of considerable interest for alterations to the structure of churches, the building of galleries and new churches. Plans may be included in the later documents. (Plate 5(c).) They also relate to monuments and private pews.

ESTATE RECORDS

Within the last few years great quantities of title-deeds and manorial documents, previously held by the Church Commissioners, have been distributed to the appropriate local repositories.

Probate Records

WILLS

Using local archives, except in a narrow field, generally involves looking at wills. To most people interested in biographical, genealogical, parochial, social and economic history, wills are a vital source, though some social and economic historians have been slow to appreciate their significance.

Even if the probate inventory (see pp. 48–49) has not survived, a will usually mentions some of the testator's goods and furniture, such as the 'second best bed' bequeathed by Shakespeare to his wife; tradesmen and farmers generally refer to some of their stock-in-trade, implements or livestock. Groups of wills lend themselves to various forms of analysis, and students may like to know that little has been done in this direction, partly because easy access and special indexes have only recently been provided. Reading wills can be an exciting pursuit: one finds a record of the testator's circle of friends; other references are sometimes surprising. But many wills are brief and prosaic, for example, the disappointingly barren will of that interesting Elizabethan, William Harrison, author of the *Description of England.* (Extracts, 9.)

Numerous wills, but representing only a small fraction of the total, have been printed in full or in abstract by local record and archaeological societies in the past century. But the greatest service to the public has been the work of the British Record Society, whose *Index Library* series now runs to more than eighty volumes. Each volume lists in alphabetical order the wills or administrations of the Prerogative Court of Canterbury (see p. 45) or one of the local courts, giving the testator's abode (parish), rank or occupation, and sometimes other brief particulars. (See details of contents of the series in the Appendix.)

Wills were proved in no less than three hundred courts! These were all ecclesiastical (except for a few lay courts, chiefly manorial), as the Church proved all wills until 1858, when secular probate registries were set up and to which the older records were transferred.

An executor usually proved a will locally in the lowest of the hierarchy of these courts – normally that of the archdeacon, but some archdeacons had no testamentary jurisdiction. If the testator's property lay in two archdeaconries or two jurisdictions, the will had to be proved in the bishop's (episcopal, or consistory) court. If the testator held in two dioceses, or his property was substantial, then probate was in the archbishop's Prerogative Court (Canterbury or York province, these two great collections of wills being known as P.C.C. and P.C.Y. respectively). Space does not allow further elaboration, but the general effect was that the wills of most testators above the rank of minor gentry are in P.C.C. or P.C.Y., not in local archives. P.C.C. are now in the Principal Probate Registry, Somerset House, Strand, London, WC2 (inquiries should be addressed to the Literary Search Department); P.C.Y. are in the Borthwick Institute of Historical Research, St. Anthony's Hall, York (inquiries to the Archivist).

Exempt from this procedure were many 'peculiars', which had their own courts, with jurisdiction over one or many parishes in one or more archdeaconries or dioceses, and held by archbishops, bishops, deans and chapters, and a small number of colleges and lords of manors. *Wills and Where to Find Them* (see p. 47) gives outline county maps showing jurisdictional boundaries and lists parishes outside the main courts.

But there are also the inhibition periods to be borne in mind. Usually a bishop's visitation of the archdeaconries in his diocese took place every three years. During the visitation the lower courts were inhibited from acting for three but occasionally four or six months, in consequence of which the wills proved in those months are to be found in the bishop's court. Finally, it must be remembered that probate of all wills was exercised by a civil commission during the Commonwealth; these were later absorbed into P.C.C. No will proved during 1653–60 is therefore to be found in the records of a local court.

This brief attempt to enlighten some aspects of the problem necessarily omits other facets, and the student can do no better, after first consulting the key already mentioned, than to examine the printed *Guide* to the local record office, if published, for further details.

The specific case of Lancashire, as an example of the confused history of probate administration, was thus cited in *Local Records : their Nature and Care*:

When the new diocese of Chester was created in 1540 its jurisdiction covered the whole of Cheshire and Lancashire south of the Ribble, as well as part of the West Riding of Yorkshire which was in the Lancashire parish of Rochdale, previously in the diocese of Coventry and Lichfield. Also brought into the new diocese was the great Archdeaconry of Richmond, previously in the diocese of York, which covered Lancashire north of the Ribble, south-west Westmorland, south-west Cumberland, western parts of the West Riding of Yorkshire, and parts of the North Riding. To add to the confusion, the western deaneries of the Archdeaconry, including north Lancashire, and the eastern deaneries were administered separately. Add to this several manorial peculiars in the Lune valley and it will be seen in how many places probate records relating to one county may be found. Indeed this is not the whole story, for to the above cited jurisdictions affecting one county must be added the Prerogative Court of York – where [among the court books and cause papers] may be found many Lancashire wills which have been the subject of dispute.

The writer might have added that Lancashire wills are also among the ordinary probate records in P.C.Y. for testators who held property in more than one diocese of the northern province.

Wills may exist in three forms – the original bearing the signatures or marks of the testators and witnesses; a registered copy with a note of probate; or a probate copy.

Court records usually include both original wills, generally on paper and folded into annual bundles, and full transcripts entered into very large registers, sometimes identified by the surname of the testator whose will is the first in the volume. (Hence 'Shaw 57', the way in which such wills have normally been cited in the past, for example, in local societies' publications, means that the will is on folio fifty-seven of the register known as 'Shaw'.) For some courts the originals are preserved from an earlier date than the registered copies; and vice versa. For others, there are gaps in one of the series. In general, there-fore, they are complementary. The probate copy was made on parch-ment, to which was attached a certificate, or letters of probate, also on parchment and usually measuring about eight by six inches, of the proving of the will and the grant of administration of the deceased's goods to the executors. Probate copies are mostly preserved in bundles of private title-deeds (p. 66).

In intestacy, letters of administration were granted by the court to the next of kin and often also to creditors. These are somewhat similar in form to letters of probate, though usually printed, with blanks for filling in the name of the administrator (or administratrix), the relation-ship being stated; the court seal is appended.

There have been very extensive changes in the custody of 'local' wills in recent years, the great majority of those proved before 1858 having been transferred to county record offices, but this is an over-simpli-fied statement. A most useful key to this labyrinth, however, is now available. *Wills and Where to Find Them*, by J. S. W. Gibson, published for the British Record Society by Phillimore, Shopwyke Hall, Chichester (1974), is in fact an invaluable guide for the novice, and he is advised to consult it before his first visit to a local repository. With the aid of this book, he will be able to recognize alleys which may prove to be blind, and set forth again quickly on a surer path. Brief details are set out in the following table, which also states where the collection does not coincide with the area of the county:

Pre-1858 local wills *not* in county record offices or
in *more than one* local repository

BERKSHIRE Dept. of Western MSS., Bodleian Library, Oxford.

CAMBRIDGESHIRE University Library, Cambridge.

CHESHIRE C.R.O., The Castle, Chester (original wills), and Lancs. R.O. Sessions House, Preston (registers).

CORNWALL C.R.O. County Hall, Truro (but those for twenty-seven parishes destroyed in 1942).

DERBYSHIRE Staffs. Joint R.O., Public Library, Lichfield, Staffs.

DURHAM Prior's Kitchen, The College, Durham.

GLOUCESTERSHIRE City Library, Gloucester.

HEREFORDSHIRE National Library of Wales, Aberystwyth.

HERTFORDSHIRE C.R.O., County Hall, Hertford (except as follows), and Essex R.O., County Hall, Chelmsford (thirty-one parishes, East Hertfordshire).

LANCASHIRE (see pp. 45–46).

NORTHAMPTONSHIRE N.R.O., Delapre Abbey, Northampton.

NORFOLK Central Library, Norwich.

NORTHUMBERLAND Prior's Kitchen, The College, Durham.

OXFORDSHIRE Dept. of Western MSS., Bodleian Library, Oxford.

RUTLAND Northants. R.O., Delapre Abbey, Northampton.

SHROPSHIRE Staffs. Joint R.O., Public Library, Lichfield.

STAFFORDSHIRE Staffs. Joint R.O., Public Library, Lichfield.

SUFFOLK Joint R.O., County Hall, Ipswich (Archd'y of Suffolk), and Joint R.O., 8 Angel Hill, Bury St Edmunds (Archd'y of Sudbury).

SURREY Principal Probate Registry, Somerset House, WC2 (may be transferred to a local authority repository in near future).

WARWICKSHIRE Staffs. Joint R.O., Public Library, Lichfield.

YORKSHIRE Borthwick Inst. of Hist. Research, St Anthony's Hall,

York (except as follows), Lancashire R.O., Sessions House, Preston (Archdeaconry of Richmond, West), and City Library, Leeds (Archdeaconry of Richmond, East).
WALES (all counties) National Library of Wales, Aberystwyth.

Students may like to know, especially if they are interested in wills of Exeter diocese which were lost by enemy action in the last war, that local record offices also have large numbers of probate copies of wills in private estate and family archives and that many wills are recited in part in manor court rolls.

INVENTORIES

Before a will was proved, the executors were obliged to get two or three neighbours to list and 'appraise' (value) the furniture, clothes, stocks and implements of the deceased's trade or craft, and other goods.

These are of such extraordinary interest (Extracts, 10 to 13) that the reader must be warned, to avoid disappointment, that his hope of using them depends on whether they have or have not survived for his diocese or archdeaconry. The sad fact is that, although for some areas they have been preserved in the thousands, others have lost nearly all these treasures. Those that have been preserved are now generally in the county (diocesan) record office, and in the absence of a printed *Guide* the county archivist will tell inquirers whether inventories for his own area are extant, and whether they have been indexed by testators and by parishes.

An inventory usually gives the deceased's parish and often his status, trade or occupation. The contents of the house are listed, room by room, usually beginning with the hall and ending with outhouses, barns, farm stock, growing crops, 'apparel', plate and jewellery, cash and debts.

It will be readily seen that inventories may in some circumstances be ideal documents for the study of dwellings and furniture as well as household, farm and craft utensils and implements, and the like. But it is seldom that existing old houses can be definitely identified with those described in inventories. Wider fields of study, where large collections of inventories are accessible, include the rise and fall of local industries and other aspects of social and economic history.

The largest series of printed inventories relate to Bedfordshire, Nottinghamshire, Cheshire, Essex, Lancashire, Lincolnshire, Newcastle, west Suffolk, and Yorkshire. A fuller list of published inventories, county by county, is in J. West, *Village Records*, pp. 129–31, which also has a long section (pp. 92–129) on Worcestershire inventories, with transcripts and plans of houses reconstructed from five inventories, an analysis of occupations, and a glossary of unusual words found in inventories. Still greater use has been made of inventories for various counties in C. W. Barley, *The English Farmhouse and Cottage*. Chapter 9, 'Fieldwork: Buildings', in W. G. Hoskins, *Local History in England*, and the Council for British Archaeology's Report III, *The Investigation of Smaller Domestic Buildings*, all invaluable. (See Appendix, 'Short Guides to Records – Probate Inventories'; also *Local Historian*, article on Inventories (1959).)

Nonconformist and Roman Catholic Records

Records of the Protestant nonconformists, including Congregationalists, Baptists, Methodists and the Society of Friends, are slowly being deposited in local record offices. Trustees are urged to ensure their preservation by allowing their older records to be given the better conditions of safety which an archive repository provides. Students are likely to find a few minute-books and account-books of each of the Free Church sects in most county record offices – adequate material perhaps for gaining a general impression of their affairs, but those desiring old records of a particular chapel may have real difficulty in tracing them, if indeed they have been preserved.

The Quakers have always been assiduous in recording their quiet activities, and their archives may also include 'suffering books', giving name and abode, nature and amount of demand, names of J.P. and constable, and value of articles distrained, compiled during the persecution period, also removal certificates or testimonials given when a member moved to another county or country, especially of course to Pennsylvania. (Plates 11(a), 13(b).) Friends' records fall into three groups: Quarterly Meetings, Monthly Meetings (smaller areas), and Particular Meetings (rare). The seventeenth-century minute-books for Buckinghamshire and Lincolnshire meetings have been printed in each case by the county record society. The best series are in the Kent R.O.

Nearly all Roman Catholic church records remain in ecclesiastical custody, but the Lancashire R.O. holds a fairly large number of registers, accounts and other documents.

The most useful account is in Chapter xxii ('Archives of the Non-Established Churches') of L. Redstone and F. W. Steer (eds.), *Local Records* (Society of Archivists). The introductions to volumes vii and viii of *Warwickshire County Records* (1946, 1953) include long sections on nonconformists and papists, 1660–1750. The long series of publications of the Catholic Record Society is a mine of information; those of the various Free Churches historical societies, though slighter, are also useful.

Charity and School Records

The archives of the thousands of village charities, if surviving, are usually found among the Parish Records (ecclesiastical or civil); those of urban charities mingled in the church records of the parish or in the official Borough Records (see pp. 35 and 61). The legal custodians of large quantities of records of other charities, not under the control of District Councils, Parochial Church or Parish Councils, are local trustees, who may or may not have entrusted the archives to a public repository.

For some ancient and substantial endowed institutions there are very large numbers of title-deeds, account-books, letters and papers, such as those of the Foundling Hospital, now in the Greater London Record Office.

Surrey is the only county for which there is a detailed catalogue (published by the County Council in 1930) of all the known extant *Records of Schools and other Endowed Institutions*, and this reveals something of the wealth of interesting documents that have survived for some of the famous charities in Surrey, such as the Trinity Hospitals at Croydon and Guildford.

In connection with the quatercentenaries of the so-called King Edward VI Grammar Schools, a number of school histories have recently appeared, and these illustrate the sort of archives which the student of the history of other ancient schools may hope to trace. For the records of British and National schools and School Boards (see p. 34).

Parish Records – Church and Civil

Except for maps, wills and inventories, parish records are the most frequently used local archives. Like County (Quarter Sessions) records, they cover a very wide field of information because of the heterogeneous nature of their contents. Approximately one in every three parishes has by now (1965) transferred some or all of its older archives to the county, diocesan or borough record office, and this process will certainly continue until the great majority of the more ancient parochial documents are in such repositories.

Although destruction and loss of the older records of many parishes is a serious matter and the consequent lack of material on some aspects of parish history can never be wholly written up from other sources, the vigorous drives by local archivists to preserve what remains has already led to hundreds of thousands of documents being safeguarded for the future student. The most effective means of securing their deposit is a comprehensive survey of parish records made by personal visits.

The colossal quantity of documents received by local repositories in the past forty years and now being added to at a rapid rate is the result of several typically English compromises. Several pieces of legislation, largely optional, provide the bases for negotiating transfers by which the archivist relieves the parish custodians of the responsibility for their proper care, and he catalogues them, repairs them if necessary, and makes them accessible to students; in some offices the more important records are microfilmed as a further security.

The Local Government Act, 1894, set up Parish Councils and Meetings to take over the civil functions of the Vestries. In theory the civil records of the parish should then have passed to the new bodies, but they mostly remained in the church or parsonage. County Councils are statutorily obliged to inquire 'from time to time' into their safe keeping. To overcome the anomaly of the civil documents still remaining in the incumbent's charge, bishops or archdeacons have been invited to sponsor inquiries, so that all parish archives including church records could be covered. Many local record repositories have been formally recognized by the bishops as diocesan record offices under the Parochial Records Measure (Church Assembly), 1929.

The description of the various classes of parish records which follows may be even more helpful to the student who finds them still in the church chest (especially if they include a mass of unsorted poor law settlement papers) than if they are fully listed in a local record office. For fuller details and copious extracts from the archives of many parishes, see W. E. Tate, *The Parish Chest: A Study of the Records of Parochial Administration in England* (revised edition 1960). Detailed catalogues of parish records have been published by the county council, county record society or diocesan authority in the case of Essex, Gloucestershire and city of Bristol, Kent, Shropshire, Somerset, Surrey and Yorkshire (East Riding); and the *Guides* to several county record offices give lists.

REGISTERS

The recording of baptisms, marriages and burials was begun in 1538 on the injunctions of Thomas Cromwell, Henry VIII's Vicar-General. In 1598 the Church ordered that all registers were to be transcribed on parchment, with the option of starting the copy in 1558. The original paper registers survive for between one and two out of every hundred parishes, and the parchment registers from 1538 or 1558 for about one in eight and one in four parishes respectively. Some of the 1598 copies are examples of fine penmanship and relatively easy to read. Many parishes have lost their seventeenth-century registers and a few have preserved none before 1754 or even 1813, the years when printed-form books for marriages, and for baptisms and burials respectively, were instituted.

A Commonwealth ordinance passed in 1653, after Oliver Cromwell had become Protector, substituted a civil parish registrar and civil marriage before a justice of the peace for the clergyman, and registration of births in place of baptism. All this was reversed at the Restoration. Many 1653–60 registers are in illiterate handwritings. Many, too, are incomplete for the Civil War and Commonwealth periods. The Burial in Woollen Act, 1678, passed to help the woollen industry, enjoined that every burial entry should include a note of the statutory affidavit, but in due course this was discontinued.

After Lord Hardwicke's Marriage Act of 1753, nearly every parish bought one of the new volumes with the prescribed spaces for the parties' and witnesses' signatures (or marks). From 1838, when civil registration of births, marriages and deaths came in, church registers are less important. Before 1754 there is little uniformity about the form of entries or their order. Baptisms, marriage and burials may be in separate sections of a register, or on alternate pages, or all in chronological order, or mixed up.

Whether entries are found to be in Latin or English before 1733 depends largely on the whim of the clergyman, and the neatness of his writing and legibility depends partly on the quality of his ink. Scribbled and almost unreadable pages are more commonly seen in eighteenth-

and late seventeenth-century registers than in those of earlier date. Whatever the period being read, inaccurate guessing of names must be rigorously avoided where the handwriting is difficult. Careful copying of letters of which the student is in no doubt in order to construct the scribe's alphabet will amply repay the trouble and will pinpoint peculiar letters (see p. 6).

At the beginning of many registers before 1812, and a few after that date, will be found miscellaneous notes about parochial affairs such as tithing customs and perambulations of the boundaries, sometimes of considerable interest.

Parish registers are invaluable sources, though with obvious qualifications, for tackling subjects of broader interest than genealogy and biography, such as the incidence of plagues, infectious diseases and epidemics, infantile mortality and longevity, illegitimacy and vagrancy, old-established families and other measures of the stability of the population, and the origin and decline of local industries. (In my series of *Bedfordshire Parish Registers* (44 vols., 1931–53) for example, the occupations revealed that market-gardening started much earlier than was previously believed.) A relatively new subject, demography, or the study of population problems, is referred to in W. G. Hoskins, *Local History in England*, pp. 142–149, is usefully dealt with in L. Munby's *Hertfordshire Population Statistics* (Phillimore for H.L.H.C.) and is being actively pursued by the Cambridge Group for the History of Population and Social Structure (20 Silver Street, Cambridge).[1]

Most of these subjects can be looked at in the registers of a single parish, but sounder results are obtained from those of a wider area, and the large number of printed copies and modern transcripts now available should encourage such work.

The ancient registers (pre-1838 or pre-1813) of two thousand or more parishes are now deposited in county (diocesan) record offices, and their number is steadily increasing. But this ratio of about one in six parishes is far from uniform throughout the country. In some counties it is much higher; in others, much lower.

Some of the clergy in the past four centuries have been negligent in looking after their ancient registers, but during the past century many devoted parsons have transcribed them as a safeguard against loss of originals, and a larger number have been copied by laymen. In recent

---

[1] See E. A. Wrigley (ed.), *Introduction to Historical Demography* (1966) and other books and articles cited by W. B. Stephens, *Sources for English Local History* (1973), pp. 23–40.

years the typewriter has produced two or more copies, one for the parish, another for the local record officer or library or for the Society of Genealogists' library. Where only one transcript was made, this should not be kept with the original but in the parsonage or preferably in the diocesan record office if the incumbent desires to keep the original register.

The pre-1813 or pre-1755 registers of some hundreds of parishes have been published, mostly by county parish register societies. Here again there is wide variation between counties and between fulness of editing and indexing. The Bedfordshire series is somewhat exceptional in that original registers and bishop's transcripts were fully collated throughout, as a result of which many thousands of entries and additional facts not in the registers were incorporated in the series.

The marriages (only) for a large number of parishes were printed in county volumes by Messrs Phillimore between 1900 and 1927, but they are not indexed. The largest collection of modern register copies (printed, typescript and manuscript) is in the possession of the Society of Genealogists, 37 Harrington Gardens, London, sw7, which has published a list of these and a separate list of all other known copies.

Parish registers are virtually the only local archives for which a production fee may be charged, the amount depending on the period to be searched. While most clergymen are willing to waive or reduce their legal fees for the genuine student, he should be warned that the fee chargeable for a long search could be prohibitive and if not levied a small donation should be offered.

RATES AND OTHER LISTS

It is surprising how few people are aware that the information required from parish registers can often be enlarged from other parish records, some of which may add interesting details. At the lowest level, there are for most parishes various lists of names which will amplify the bare facts in the registers, and even if time is limited these lists may repay inquiry.

The commonest are the assessments for parochial rates – for the church, the poor and the roads; less frequently, for the constables and the militia, or 'lighting and watching' in later years. Where a parish has lost its earliest register there is a chance that a few rate-lists even of late sixteenth century date have survived. (Plate 2(b).) Later lists vary greatly in the detail given. Against each ratepayer's name the sum is always stated. Additional facts may include the annual value (rental) of the property, the previous occupier, and a bare note to identify the property, such as 'Hill Farm', 'George Inn, 'house', or 'plantation'. (Plate 17(b).) The lists are essentially those of occupiers, who may or may not have been the owners; but after 1834 both owners and occupiers are invariably given in the poor rate-books. (See Appendix, 'Short Guides to Records – Rate Books'.)

Lists of men liable to serve in the militia are occasionally found. Of more importance are the parochial schedules dealing with preparations against threatened invasion during the French Wars similar to those sometimes found in the County Records (p. 32).

Incumbents' vested interest in tithes led some to keep notebooks setting out the names of the tithepayers, with those of the farms and even the fields. They may turn up for almost any period between about 1600 and the date of the parish tithe award (p. 41).

VESTRY MINUTES ('Parish books')

The ancient meeting of the parishioners which levied the church rate, named after the church vestry where they assembled, assumed more importance when Tudor legislation imposed responsibility for the poor and the roads on the parish. It is not true, however, as some historians state, that the growing influence of the vestry lay in its taking over most of the functions of the manor court everywhere in this period. The evidence of court rolls of some manors proves clearly that certain manors indeed became more active between about 1550 and 1660. There was in fact much overlapping in the administrative and penal jurisdiction of Quarter Sessions, the bishop's (or archdeacon's) court, the vestry and the manor court. The repair (or lack of repair) of roads and bridges, for example, was dealt with by manor court, vestry and Quarter Sessions; absence from church was presented either to the Church court or Quarter Sessions; and certain minor offences might come before any of these four bodies.

It is rare to discover minute- or memoranda-books dating from before the second half of the sixteenth century, when the parish became the unit for the upkeep of the roads and the relief of the poor. At this early date, some did not bother to record in a book officers' appointments or to copy their loose sheets of rough accounts into it. Such a 'parish book' or 'town book'[1], where extant, may only give the

[1] Not until the eighteenth century did the old term 'town', meaning village, disappear; 'town' then gradually became the short term for market town.

briefest summary of the officers' annual accounts, in fact merely the total income from the rate and the total expenditure. But if a more detailed book exists it may provide a vivid chronicle of parish affairs, and even by the early seventeenth century such a record is among the most informative and illuminating sources for the student of local history. The Sturges Bourne Act of 1819 empowered parishes to form a Select Vestry, whose minutes are usually fuller than those of an Open Vestry. The former are mostly confined to populous parishes. (Plate 18(a).) In the north of England the extensive parishes were mostly divided into their independent townships for civil purposes.

An important aspect of civil parish records between 1689 and 1834 is that this was the only period in English history when the central government took little trouble over local affairs: each parish and township therefore has an individual story.

Some vestry minutes have been published, e.g. for Liverpool, Kettering, Wimbledon and Barking.

After the Guardians took over the overseers' chief duties in 1834, the minutes of the vestry suddenly shrank in length unless the parish was an urban one or in a rapidly growing industrial area, when the vestry's new problems gave it other business to record – new roads, the impact of railways, fire engines, and public health. Some populous parishes, not under a Town Council or Board of Health, found it necessary to appoint committees, which started separate minutes or various new registers.

Post-1834 vestry records of urban parishes, if not in the custody of the county archivist, are mostly in the custody of the town clerk or the borough archivist or librarian. As important source material for social and economic history, these relatively modern vestry minutes have not received the attention which they deserve. In connection with parallel records such as those of the Highway Boards or Poor Law Unions, the post-1834 vestry minutes of an important parish provide a suitable subject for trainee teachers, and those of some or all the parishes within a Union, for post-graduate students. (Extracts, 8.)

CHURCHWARDENS

Pre-Reformation churchwardens' accounts are extant for about one per cent of English parishes. Elizabethan churchwardens' accounts exist for perhaps twice that percentage. In that and the following century, the items of expenditure faithfully mirror the swings of the politico-religious pendulum. (Plate 2(a) and Extracts 1 and 2.) More important is the evidence of structural and other alterations in the church. Erection of galleries in the eighteenth century and 'restoration' (so called) in the following century may be precisely dated from the accounts. Most of the entries of course deal with routine expenses such as communion wine, bell ropes and cleaning. Churchwardens' accounts, especially those of early date, have been printed for many parishes, e.g. for Lambeth, 1504–1645 (Surrey Rec. Soc., 1940), which has a scholarly introduction.

The office of churchwarden was the most substantial of the four chief parochial offices: each was usually held by two people for one year, and in many parishes they were elected on a rough-and-ready rota system, the farmers, for instance, usually serving as churchwardens in turn. All were unpaid, and in the case of constables, surveyors and overseers mostly unskilled and unwilling, some almost illiterate – points to bear in mind in reading the records they have left behind them. Under the Poor Law Acts, churchwardens were nominally joined with overseers for poor relief. They were also responsible for the simple fire-fighting equipment which was stored in churches for communal use (Plate 6(a)) and for making payments for the destruction of 'noyfull fowles and vermyn', which included not only crows, rooks and sparrows, but also moles and foxes.

CONSTABLES

From medieval times until an Act of 1842 the annual appointment of the petty constable was legally the responsibility of the court leet held by the lord of the manor, but in some manors the courts were not held annually, and the constables (usually two) were chosen or elected by the parishioners and then sworn before justices of the peace in Petty Sessions. Constables' accounts may refer to the repair of the archery butts and the 'arms' which each parish had to provide under an Act of 1558; the entries may mention calivers, guns, gunpowder and match, pikes, swords, corselets, head pieces and soldiers' coats. There may be an incidental mention of the Civil War or movements of troops in later periods. Constables' records, however, are mostly concerned with rogues and vagabonds, and their accounts include frequent items for relieving 'passengers', i.e. travellers having an official pass. Account books for constables' expenses were never started in the smaller parishes, and the overseers having reimbursed them often preserved their scrappy sheets among the poor relief papers.

SURVEYORS OF THE HIGHWAYS

The Highways Act of 1555 obliged every parish annually to elect two surveyors of highways, or waywardens, and to assess every adult according to his station to provide cartage or labour, later known as 'statute labour', in lieu of which in later years many paid fines or compositions out of which payments for digging gravel, picking stones, filling in ruts and so forth were made. Such rudimentary maintenance scarcely demanded much in the way of account-books in the early days, and they are indeed rarely met with before the early eighteenth century. (Extracts 3 and 4, pp. 85–6.) Commutation was regularized by Acts of 1766 and 1773. Surveyors' books may therefore contain disbursements, rate-lists and composition-lists. In later years and before the creation of Highway Boards (p. 34) there is evidence that some of the more populous parishes tried interesting road-maintenance experiments, but main roads had mostly come under the control of Turnpike Trusts (p. 33).

OVERSEERS OF THE POOR

Records of the relief of the poor in some parishes consist of many account-books and hundreds, even thousands, of papers. Whilst most readers know that the Poor Law Acts of 1597–1601 ordered the appointment of two overseers of the poor each year in every parish, it may be recalled that legislation in 1563 and 1573 compelled parishioners to contribute to the relief of impotent paupers, and archivists are gradually discovering more and more of the rare records of this early period or recognizing as accounts of the pre-1597 'collectors of the poor' what were previously thought to be churchwardens' accounts. From 1601 to the great Poor Law Amendment Act of 1834 the ever-growing problem of poor relief gave rise to a rapidly increasing quantity of documents.

Overseers' accounts and vestry minutes tell of the diverse ways in which each parish tackled the question independently of its neighbours. Simple, direct relief of the poor lay in monthly or weekly payments to the aged, impotent, sick and orphans, or to goodwives for looking after them. By the eighteenth century other methods were tried. A poorhouse was acquired in which most of the poor were placed; or a workhouse and material for the poor to be employed on were provided in an attempt to get the inmates to produce some income; or a contract was made with a local man willing to relieve the lazy overseers of the bother, either for so much a head or for a lump sum, with all its scope for abuses; or some further variation of these or similar expedients. Common sense prevailed upon Parliament to pass Local Acts from 1696 onwards by which the overseers of the numerous parishes in some of the cities and larger boroughs were superseded by Incorporated Guardians of the Poor, who set up joint borough workhouses or houses of industry. Gilbert's Act of 1782 empowered rural parishes to unite with the object of setting up reformed kinds of workhouses; sixty-seven unions comprising nine hundred and twenty-four parishes were established.

Until well into the nineteenth century the relief of the poor was so wide in conception that it embraced most of present social services in a rudimentary way. Medical attention was provided in a variety of ways. Overseers' disbursements include many payments to local doctors and midwives. It is not unusual to find that the payment of the balance of a doctor's fee was conditional on a cure! There is seen a natural tendency to pay an annual fee a 'surgeon and apothecary', especially after about 1700, for dealing with all the parish poor. In later years contracts for mass inoculation against smallpox afford clear evidence of local epidemics; such treatment was of course superseded subsequently by vaccination.

Unlike churchwardens' accounts, which have been edited by learned antiquaries, very few overseers' records have been printed, but some have been well drawn upon, e.g. those for Eaton Socon and Woodford (Beds. Hist. Rec. Soc. and Woodford Hist. Soc.). (Extracts, 5.)

In scores of parishes there still lies, crushed at the bottom of the ancient parish chest or hidden in a dark corner of a cupboard in the vestry, the belfry or the parsonage, a mass of old papers, sometimes in folded bundles, more often loose, crumpled and dirty. If the parish had become populous by 1800 or thereabouts the number of such documents may run to several thousands. Their preservation, despite the vicissitudes to which they have been subject, is extraordinary: changes of incumbents, churchwardens, parish clerks; interregna in which anyone with a zeal for tidying up might have felt justified or even constrained to turn out such apparent rubbish. But life moves faster nowadays, and the risk of what has survived being destroyed in the near future, before being collected by the county or city archivist, is a serious one. Every reader, clerical or lay, knowing the existence of such papers is urged to inform the local archivist, for they are part of the documentary material for the history of our country during the period before 1834 when the social services were administered by about fifteen thousand separate parishes or townships.

Pathetic, scrawled applications for parochial relief in money or kind (Plate 18(b)), scrappy little receipts for the same, tradesmen's receipted bills for food and other necessaries for workhouse or poorhouse, and various other documents may be embedded in the annual bundle of the overseers' bills and vouchers submitted for approval to the vestry. Occasionally one finds a printed billhead, perhaps with an engraving of the local inn or grocer's or draper's shop.

Or the parish papers may be the vivid reminders of the operation of the long series of Acts of Parliament known as the settlement laws. (Plate 23.) Even before the Settlement Act of 1662 a few parishes took action against 'intruders', mostly where the manor court was inactive. By this Act the vestry through its overseers of the poor became responsible for removing paupers or potential paupers to their 'place of settlement' on the order of two justices of the peace. The Act defined the four qualifications for gaining a parish settlement, which were birth, payment of rates on property assessed at or over ten pounds a year, completing a full year as a hired servant, or serving the full term as an apprentice. Two copies of the justices' order of removal were made, one for each parish. The 1662 Act authorized the issue of a certificate by the parish in which a man was settled to the parish in which he hoped to take up his abode. By such an indemnity certificate the receiving parish could be relieved of financial liability in the event of the immigrant's becoming chargeable. (See also Extracts, 6, 7.)

Before a removal order was approved by the justices a statement was taken from the pauper. These written 'examinations' in the case of anyone who had moved about a good deal are like miniature auto-biographies; they furnish place of birth and marriage and brief details of employments. Apprenticeship of pauper children, especially orphans, to the age of twenty-one (or marriage, for a girl) was a sound enough principle in social welfare, intended to give the child a trade or craft. But it opened the way to various abuses, providing instead a way by which a mean vestry could rid the parish from all liability for future maintenance by apprenticing to a master elsewhere (perhaps a north country millowner), or a low-grade substitute for a trade by apprenticing within the parish to 'husbandry' or 'housewifery' which might amount merely to unskilled, menial farm or domestic service. A simple analysis of surviving indentures may show whether the vestry had any moral conscience in trying to set up their young paupers in a skilled occupation or not.

CHARITIES

For most parishes there are records of ancient charitable endowments such as the original deed or probate copy of the founder's will or deeds of appointment of new trustees. Of more interest are account-books giving each year the income with details of how it was spent, e.g. on up-keep of the church guildhall or poorhouse, repairing the roads or a bridge, maintaining a school or apprenticing children to a satisfactory trade, providing loaves or coal, or merely cash distributions. (See also p. 50.) (Extracts, 1.)

MISCELLANEOUS

The church chest was the only parochial repository, and into it were placed various other records of parochial affairs, especially those which arose in the nineteenth century, such as voluntary fire brigades, water and sanitary services, lighting, watching and paving inspectors, medical, clothing, coal and provident clubs and societies. The most extraordinary documents may turn up in parish records. In Essex, for example, were found records of the 'Aveley Lunatick Clubb', 1763–64, which met on the first Monday after each full moon, and a deed of sale of a longboat, the 'Prophet of Cannoden', 1709.

PARISH COUNCIL MINUTES

Parish Councils were set up in 1894, and a few of the earlier minute-books are now deposited in county record offices. Clerks to some Parish Councils are willing to allow history students to look at their older minutes.

Estate and Family Archives

'The archives of great estates of old landed families offer the historian invaluable and unusually diverse material. Accumulated without pre-meditation or design, in the administration of the private and business concerns of men and women of property – and consequently of influence both in public and local affairs – they portray, in most intimate detail, the everyday activities of small social groups – manor, estate, or domestic circle. This type of record, therefore, makes a helpful contribution to the understanding of the English people. It inevitably reflects also the impact of national events upon ordinary people, revealing the Englishman as he lived and laboured alike in times of triumph or disaster, concord or controversy, plenty or want.'[1]

[1] *Guide to the Essex Record Office* (revd. edn., 1969, p. 89).

[61]

The term Estate and Family Archives has been fairly generally adopted by local archivists, but the description in a local record office *Guide* of what appears to be a single collection may in fact represent editorial merging, for the student's convenience, of archives received from more than one source – the family muniment-room, the London and country solicitors' and estate agents' offices, 'strays' secured through the good services of the British Records Association and the Historical Manuscripts Commission, and so forth.[1] Some of the sources are probably quite separate in the typescript catalogues from the main group.

The subjects on which estate and family archives may yield material are virtually unlimited. In the following pages we try to describe the classes very commonly found in the catalogues of local record offices.

ESTATE MAPS

Well-drawn, detailed and accurate estate maps are the greatest treasures for the local historian, especially if they are of early date and cover a large area, for a single manuscript map of a whole parish may give clearly more topographical information than is contained in hundreds of title-deeds and other documents. (Plates 30 to 32.)

At a rough estimate, over twenty thousand private estate maps dated before about 1850 have now been found and are accessible in local record offices and manuscript departments of libraries. This works out at an average of nearly two estate maps for every parish, in addition to which there is probably an enclosure map (p. 25) or tithe map (p. 41) or both. The great majority show small estates or only a single farm, but perhaps one in ten covers the entire parish and some portray big estates extending into several parishes. For some towns and villages there may of course be no manuscript maps of earlier date than those accompanying the tithe or enclosure awards. But old estate maps are being entrusted to archivists somewhere in England and Wales almost every day, each filling in a piece of the country's topographical history.

What does the average estate map of (say) 1750 show? Almost certainly all field boundaries, with the name and acreage of each field and wood, the roads and lanes, streams and ponds, greens and unenclosed waste. Every dwelling is shown, miniature drawings usually in block plan but sometimes of the important buildings and farmhouses are given. Colour may be used to show the land use (arable, meadow,

[1] *Idem* (chart), p. 87.

pasture, hopfield, quarry, etc.) or to distinguish the areas or ownership of farms and smaller holdings. The map of a whole parish normally names the owners and may also give the occupiers.

If the map was drawn before the date of an enclosure award of the open fields, it probably shows the owner's scattered strips; if he was a substantial landowner in the parish it may provide the whole pattern of the unenclosed lands. (Plates 28 to 30.) Other examples are in F. G. Emmison, *Types of Common-Field Parish: with Maps* (Nat. Council of Social Service, revd. 1965).

Other details will depend largely on local physical features: maps of maritime parishes may show cliffs, marshes, saltings or seawalls, beaches with high and low watermarks, wild-duck decoys, coastal defence fortifications, ferries, oyster-layings and beacons; maps of upland parishes show the moors, combes and quarries; tithe maps may mark iron-workings, coal-mines, tin-mines and other industrial sites are of special interest.

Surveyors who mapped the estates of wealthy clients delight the present-day student's eye with accurate representation of the features of parks, ornamental gardens and waters, even grottoes and icehouses, often revealing delicate and accurate draughtsmanship. Among other features usually drawn in some detail are churches, chapels, windmills (careful scrutiny may reveal post-mill, smock-mill or tower-mill), watermills (fulling-mill, tidal-mill, and other types), inns (even their signs), guildhalls, schools, almshouses, workhouses, dovecotes and pounds. Woodlands are usually drawn accurately, with ridings and glades; deciduous and conifer trees may be distinguished; in parklands and even in ordinary pastures scattered trees may be individually drawn and their species indicated. Roads are generally given careful treatment; roadside verge may be distinguished from carriageways. Much attention was paid to careful delineation of parish boundaries and boundary marks ('cross on tree' and so forth) and to detached parts of parishes.

When the hard-working student wants a restful change from buildings and fields he may be able to turn his eyes, if he is lucky, to the decoration on the map – the coloured compass-rose and scale, the full heraldic achievement of the estate owner's arms, and the cartouche in which the surveyor or draughtsman pleased himself, or wished to please his employer, with ornaments and pictures of floral, geometrical, baroque, classical, allegorical, or imaginative design, cornucopia, cherubs, ruined castles, fabulous animals and other humorous or grotesque creations.

For towns and industrial places, the wealth of detail shown on large-scale manuscript maps may be of paramount importance to the student of urban history, and he should make a thorough inquiry to find out if such a map exists especially if there is more than one record office, library, museum or historical society in his area.

Printed *catalogues of maps* continue to appear slowly, and these usually include enclosure and tithe award, public schemes (canals, railways, turnpike roads, etc.) and other official maps, as well as private estate maps. They can be consulted for Bedfordshire (1930), Essex (1947), with two later supplements, and West Sussex (1962); also for Berkshire and Lancashire (enclosure maps only), and most local record office *Guides* list them more briefly. All such maps have at least been catalogued (and indexed under parishes) in typescript or manuscript in every local repository, and long searches should be unnecessary.

Maps are so vital that it seems desirable to mention that the National Repositories in London, Oxford and Cambridge have large numbers relating to private estates, and photographs can be obtained at moderate prices.

Not many reproductions of estate maps are available for study but some for Bedfordshire (especially pre-enclosure 'strip' maps), Huntingdonshire, Wiltshire, and a few other counties have been published. (For printed County Maps, see p. 71.)

SURVEYS

As silver is to gold, so is a survey, or written description of an estate, to a map: less precious but valuable; and if no contemporary map exists the survey may be detailed enough to tempt the keen student to plot the information and thus try to construct his own map. Most surveys relate to a manor, not a whole parish. Some describe the lord's demesne only (park, home farm or the like); the majority deal with the freeholds, copyholds and leaseholds and may cover a large acreage.

The best surveys give for each field its name and acreage, and, in order to identify its situation, the names of the adjacent fields; dwellings may be related to roads and lanes. The tenant's name is invariably given. A very full survey may thus give some facts not in a map. The sequence of entries is usually that of the route of the surveyor or manorial jury, proceeding from field to field, or down each street or lane. Many places and fields referred to are readily identifiable to anyone with a fair knowledge of his parish, and the jigsaw puzzle is a challenging and often rewarding one, even if some unplaceable bits remain over in the attempt to plot the survey.

Most manorial surveys belong to between about 1550 and 1700. Within that period, they may go into minute particulars, extending perhaps into three hundred pages, in Latin and English. Sometimes surveys of many manors belonging to one owner are written in a massive volume of one thousand pages or more. Before about 1550 surveys are much less likely to give all the particulars which enable fields to be located at the present time, and the document may call itself a terrier or an extent. (See Appendix, 'Short Guides to Records – Estate Maps and Surveys'.)

A terrier or rental is usually still briefer and may give no more than the field, cottage (perhaps with its name) and the manorial tenant (usually distinguishing between freeholder and copyholder). A relatively modern rental may also name the actual occupier, if not the same as the manorial tenant or owner.

MANORIAL

'Court rolls (leet only), original presentments, steward's waste, draft minutes, extents, surveys and quit rentals, bailiff's accounts.' All these terms occur, time after time, in catalogues of manorial documents. The records themselves may provide information of the utmost importance for parochial, topographical, genealogical, social, economic and agricultural history, so a brief explanation of what appears to be archivists' but is really lawyers' jargon will be useful.

In the post-medieval period manor court proceedings relate to two kinds of courts. Broadly, the Court Leet and View of Frankpledge elected the manorial officers such as constable, ale-tasters, haywards, common drivers, and until towards the end of the seventeenth century dealt with petty misdemeanours and nuisances. The Court Baron was mainly concerned with changes in tenancy of copyholds, with minor infringements of property rights, and with the regulation of open fields and meadows, and commons, heaths and greens. It was a non-penal jurisdiction. (Extracts, 14 to 16, pp. 94–98.)

TITLE-DEEDS

The archives of an estate may contain only a few old deeds, but fifty thousand or more *may* have been preserved. Taking a simple unit such as an ordinary farm with farmhouse and a few cottages, the bundle(s) of deeds probably include conveyances (purchase deeds, known by various technical terms referred to later), probate copies of wills, marriage settlements, mortgages, leases, admissions and surrenders of copyholds, etc., and perhaps an abstract of title reciting still older deeds.

Thousands of farms have deeds going back to the seventeenth century; for some the deeds are extant from the fifteenth century or even earlier; but the chance that the oldest is an unknown late Saxon charter is about one in a million. On the other hand the reader should be encouraged by the fact that local repositories already hold several million deeds dated before about 1850.

The properties described in deeds range from the smallest cottage or plot to vast estates, and may include specific references to inns, alms-houses, chapels, mills, ferries, markets, shops, maltings, foreshore rights and fisheries, dovecotes, advowsons, deer-parks, warrens, and duck-decoys. The amount of description given also varies widely. The big estate may be described merely by the names of the constituent manors and the parishes concerned; or more fully by the names of the individual farms and chief properties parish by parish, with or without their total acreages and occupiers; or by the names of every building and field; or may be so detailed as to give even the adjoining properties (and their owners), and other features, for the purpose of identification. These 'bounds' or 'abuttals' are a very useful source for names of roads, lanes and ways of every kind, bridges, commons and greens, streams and marshland drains, islands and creeks, marshes and sea-walls, springs and wells, and objects now of antiquarian interest such as wayside crosses. The state of cultivation of each parcel of land (whether arable, meadow, pasture, marsh, wood, etc.) may be indicated. Deeds rarely contain plans before 1840, and as there were no official maps giving field-numbers at that time, the difficulty of confirming the identification of any specific property may be overcome by resort to contemporary official, parish and estate maps and surveys.

You may be lucky enough to find that some or all of the old deeds in which you are interested have been calendared in detail by the record office or library. On the other hand a deed or a whole bundle may be catalogued only in a line or two, such as 'Deeds (37) of Fernhall Farm, 1590–1840'. If so and if you have little experience in reading old hand-writing and your Latin is shaky, follow the general recommendations put forward in an earlier chapter and work through the deeds back-wards, as the places, fields and parties named in the older deeds will be easier to recognize in archaic guise after you have met them in more modern forms. In a bundle of title-deeds there are usually some links in the parties' names, as the vendor recorded in the deed of, for example, 1640 may be the purchaser (or purchaser's father, or other relation) in the preceding deeds of, for example, 1610.

But these simple suggestions may prove insufficient aids in themselves if the bundle contains examples of one or another of the long obsolete and at first sight forbidding documents known as Feoffment, Bargain and Sale Enrolled, Demise, Release, Exemplification of a Common Recovery, or Final Concord (Plate 22). Several inexpensive pamphlets designed to help those wishing to read old deeds have recently been published, viz. *How to Read Old Title Deeds*, by J. Cornwall (University of Birmingham, Dept. of Extra-Mural Studies) and *Title Deeds*, by A. A. Dibben (Historical Association, 1968).

ACCOUNTS

Family archives usually include accounts. These may be limited to a single book of housekeeping expenses (Plate 21), perhaps written in a slovenly or illiterate hand, or, in the case of old-established tradesmen or farmers, to several books in which are merged items of personal and business affairs (see also p. 70). On the other hand, the control and management of a large estate necessitated the keeping of more elaborate accounts of income and expenditure, which grow in size and variety of form from the composite estate, household and personal volumes of Tudor times to the diverse ledgers, journals and so on, which the more complex management and audit of Victorian times demanded. Household accounts of the sixteenth and seventeenth centuries of substantial families of Essex and Hertfordshire have been extensively drawn upon in my *Tudor Food and Pastimes* and R. L. Hine's *Relics of an Un-Common Attorney* respectively.

The accounts may be analysed under various heads of income and expenditure, such as rents, mineral royalties and sales of stock, timber and agricultural produce and fuel on the one hand and buildings and household and wages on the other. In rare cases the original bills and vouchers may have survived. For Audley End, Essex, for example, the Essex R.O. holds nearly forty thousand covering the period 1765–1832, folded and endorsed 'glazier', 'ironmonger', 'smith', 'bricklayer', 'carpenter', 'pleasure grounds', 'travelling', 'game', 'dogs', 'ammunition', 'stables', 'poultry', 'coal', 'saddler', and so forth; these were all made up into neat, monthly bundles.

LEGAL

Few families in the course of several generations have been able to keep their affairs out of the lawcourts especially if their property is a farm or a bigger estate. Until comparatively recent years, most legal actions came before the central courts (Chancery, King's Bench, Exchequer or Common Pleas). In the seventeenth and eighteenth centuries the country gentleman seems to have been especially prone to start litigation, despite the high costs involved. Although the original records or contemporary enrolments of most of these actions are housed in the Public Record Office, copies were usually made for the parties and are commonly found in estate archives. They were generally written on paper, and, as fees were payable partly according to their length, many records of lawsuits seem to be interminable to the present-day reader. Written on foolscap, they were then folded lengthwise twice (or once only if their bulk was too thick to fold again) and endorsed with a note of the parties, the court, the date and perhaps also the technical name of the document.

OFFICIAL

Hopes of discovering in private hands great accumulations of the official papers of the older or the younger Pitt, Thomas or Oliver Cromwell, or other notable statesmen have dwindled in the past twenty years or so. The general awakening of interest and the activities of local archivists and the National Register of Archives have led to the opening nearly everywhere of storerooms seen by the officers of the Historical Manuscripts Commission in earlier years. But if the student's quest is for the personal records of less important members of parliament, an admiral, a merchant, or a North American or Indian official, a bishop, a sheriff, or a justice of the peace, a turnpike trustee, or merely a church-warden – the men who conducted the more routine affairs of the empire, the nation, the county or the parish – some of his 'official' papers will probably turn up in the family archives. Several documents of this kind are illustrated. (Plates 3, 7 and 26.)

ECCLESIASTICAL AND CHARITABLE

Many families who acquired monastic estates at the Dissolution inherited some of their manuscripts. Later 'ecclesiastical' papers in family archives relate chiefly to tithes, church chancels or presentations to benefices, arising from ownership of lay rectories or advowsons.

Some families' philanthropy led to the creation of large numbers of documents, especially where they retained control as charity trustees or where their descendants disputed the terms of the endowment in interminable lawsuits. Records of endowed schools may thus be found: the original charter of the King Edward VI Grammar School, Chelmsford, which had been 'lost' for two centuries, was quite naturally 'discovered' in the archives of Lord Petre in 1939, Sir William Petre, his ancestor, having been governor and first-named trustee.

MISCELLANEOUS

Some families have preserved thousands of quite old letters. Unluckily archivists seldom have time to list letters in detail. They may therefore prove invaluable as an untapped source. (Plates, 25, 26. Extracts, 17.)

Old diaries differ greatly in the nature of their contents. Many are travel diaries describing journeys or holidays in Britain; even diaries of the Grand Tour taken by the young heir apparent are fairly common. Diaries recording local affairs, especially those of a merchant, schoolmaster, parson, farmer, or magistrate, are rarer, but are still turning up. (Extracts, 18.) *Some Bedfordshire Diaries* (Pub. Beds. Hist. Rec. Soc., xl, 1960) brings together a dozen assorted diaries 1688–1895, mostly discovered by the oldest county record office in the past thirty years and giving an entertaining cross-section of local affairs.

Among the more colourful family archives are heraldic manuscripts – grants of arms and pedigree rolls, often 'illuminated'; with these may be linked biographical and genealogical notes sometimes extending into full (unpublished) family histories. Likewise there may be literary or antiquarian papers, of varying quality, or medical or cookery recipe books, of doubtful efficacy or extravagant taste.

Virtually anything may turn up in the muniment-room or the deed-box holding private and family archives. In so far as anything in a 'miscellaneous' category is typical, the following brief entry from the *Guide to the Nottinghamshire County Record Office* (1960), p. 100, illustrates what may be expected:

'EDGE (family of STRELLEY) . . . Miscellaneous. Timber and Forest, c. 1675–1805 (16). Notts. Parliamentary Election Poll books, 1710, 1722 and election addresses, 1796–1806 (15). Prisoners and sentences at Notts. Assizes, 1790–1905 (15). Nottingham Riots, 1679, 1831. Apprenticeship indentures, 1656, 1681. Cookery books and recipes, c. 1740 (4). Almanacks, pamphlets and advertisements, 1733–1850 (20). Newspapers, 1790–1808 (23). Willoughby Hospital, Cossal (correspondence), 1809–13 (5).'

Shortage of space in his *Guide* compels the archivist to be terse. The reader may like to refresh his memory with the wider list of subjects given on pp. 1–2.

Business Records

Land being the chief commodity until recent times and agriculture the chief industry, most of the estate archives already described are also business records. In the more limited sense and on a humbler scale are farmers' account-books, which are quite common from the eighteenth century onwards, and millers', blacksmiths' and grocers' accounts relatively so. But inquiries for tradesmen's accounts of a particular village may prove barren, and readers who learn of the existence of old account-books of small businesses are asked to notify the local archivist before they are thrown away as 'obsolete'. An insight into interesting aspects of town or village affairs may reward the student who masters the awful scrawl confronting him in a typical book. Or he may find something out of the ordinary, such as the record of expenditure of every voyage made by 'The Farmer's Delight', an Essex coastal sailing barge.

The older archives of larger businesses are gradually being entrusted to local repositories. Mergers and take-overs, as well as wartime and peacetime salvage, space-saving drives and removal to new premises, have all combined to jeopardize their preservation, and 'discovery' by their owners may unfortunately be followed by destruction. A telephone call to the nearest county or borough record office,[1] would ensure immediate advice or a visit from the archivist. As few repositories have no more space to waste than companies, the latter may rest assured that the archivist will normally not recommend retention of useless records; but if the archives are likely to prove of value to the local or economic historian he will certainly try to provide room for them if the company cannot do so. Students should realize of course that some of the more recent or confidential documents thus transferred may not yet be open to examination.

Some old-established London businesses, such as Twinings, Whit-bread and Company, and Hoare's Bank have for many years realized the historical importance of their archives, and others in the Midlands, the North, or South Wales have arranged for memoirs or solid histories

[1] If in London, where risk of loss is especially great, to the Greater London Council Record Office, Westminster Bridge.

to be prepared and printed privately or in conjunction with the local record office. (Plate 20.)

Instances occur of quite old and forgotten business records turning up in estate and family archives in the provinces, to which a successful city merchant moved perhaps a century or more ago, taking them with him to his country mansion. (Plate 12, 14(c), 16. Extracts, 19.) The ledgers of members of the du Cane family, London merchants engaged in trade with Russia and Italy, 1694–1751, thus came to light in this way in a farm barn near their Essex park. The early volumes are written in French, but the pious merchant frequently ended a satisfactory profit-statement with *Laus Deo!* A fine series of a clothier's (cloth manufacturer's) accounts, 1743–1820, was recently found in a drawer in an Essex farmhouse.

Before 1964 the Essex Record Office had received few 'modern' business records, but in the past year it was entrusted with the older archives of Bentall and Company, agricultural implement makers (from 1808), Samuel Courtauld and Company, textile manufacturers, from which the international company originated (from 1809), and John Sadd and Company, timber merchants (from 1799).

Investments by ancestors in land abroad, especially in North America and the colonies, has left many marks in family archives and official records. (Plate 14(a), (b).) As more and more are entrusted to local record offices, even distant echoes of early settlement in New England and Virginia can be expected to add to our knowledge of this exciting period.

Printed and Pictorial Collections

It is not generally realized that local record offices also house large quantities of printed material, such as auctioneers' *sale particulars* of estates, often with maps attached, which are of value in bridging gaps between modern O.S. maps or directories and old deeds. The same re-mark applies to *topographical engravings, watercolours and other original drawings, photographs,* early picture postcards, and the like, often amount-ing to scores for a given village. Students should not fail to inquire about such collections, as they often supply the means of illustrating essays and theses. Most offices also have fairly large series of early printed county maps (two good collections in the Warwickshire and Essex R.O.s, were recently catalogued and printed by the respective county councils). Even more important are complete, or nearly complete, sets of the various editions of the one-inch, six-inch and twenty-five-inch O.S. maps – *The Historian's Guide to Ordnance Survey Maps* (N.C.S.S.). helps to sort out their complexities.

Transcripts

This term, now being adopted by many local record offices, covers copies, abstracts, extracts, photographs, microfilms and catalogues of archives of local interest, the originals of which are not in the repository, e.g. modern transcripts of manor court rolls in the Public Record Office or in private custody, or of parish registers.

V

Transcripts of
Selected Illustrations

Note. Letters omitted in the original MSS. are supplied below in square brackets. In some of these transcripts superscript letters in the originals are printed, to aid the reader, above the line; in others, on the line. Editors of such MSS. should not use the former method, and unless a literal transcript is necessary should normally omit brackets.

1 (a) Deposition, Guildford Borough Court: cricket and bear-baiting, 1598

M[emorandum] that att this day came John Derrick of Gulde-forde aforesaid gent[leman] one of the Queenes Ma[jes]t[ies] Coroners of the county of Surrey beinge of the age of Fifty and nyne yeeres or thereabout[es] And voluntarily sworne and examined saith upon his oath that hee hath knowen the p[ar]cell of land lately vsed for a garden and sometime in the occupac[i]on of John Parvishe late of Guldeford aforesaid Inhoulder deceased lyinge in the p[ar]ishe of the holy Trinity in Guldeford afore-said betweene the garden somtymes Thomas Northall on the north p[ar]te and the high way leadinge through the north Towne ditch of the said Towne of Guldeford on the south p[ar]te for the space of Fyfty yeeres and more, And did knowe that the same lay waste and was vsed and occupied by the Inhabitant[es] of Guldeford aforesaid to lay Timber in and for Sawpitt[es] and for makinge of Frames of Timber for the said Inhabitant[es] And that ould Butler a Carpenter deceased dwellinge in the Towne aforesaid did Comonly vse to make frames of Timber there, And also this depon[en]t saith that hee being a Scholler in the Free Schoole of Guldeford hee and diu[er]se of his fellowes did runne and play there at Creckett and other Plaies And also that the same was vsed for the Bay-tinge of Beares in the said Towne untill the said John Parvishe did inclose the said p[ar]cell of land.

[73]

1 (b) Presentment, Essex Quarter Sessions: unlawful football, 1599

We presente that Thomas Whistock of White Notlye with nyne other of his fellowes the xxvth day of february in the xljth yere of her Ma[jes]^{tis} rayne beinge the sabaothe day did play at an vnlawfull game called the fote bale wheron grew bludshedd contrary to her Ma[jes]^{tis} peace.

2 (a) Churchwardens' expenses, St Saviour, Southwark, 1552-53

Crystemas quartar anno. vj^{to} E vj^{ti} [6th year of Edw. VI]

It[e]m for iij com[m]vnyon bokes for the quyre of the laste translatyon	xij s
It[e]m gyven in rewarde to a preacher	xx d
It[e]m for a cytation for theym that wolde not paye their tythes	xij d
It[e]m to the sompno[u]^r for s[er]uyng of yt	xij d
It[e]m to the procto[u]^r for his fee	iij s iiij d
It[e]m for wasshyng	ij s vj d
It[e]m to the po[o]^r fellowe Roger	ij s vj d
It[e]m for oyle and bromes	xvj d
It[e]m for wyne	x s
It[e]m for brede to com[m]vnycate w[i]thall	ij s
It[e]m paid to the Receavo[u]^r of the bysshop of Wynchesto[u]^r for the halfe yeres rente of the p[ar]sonage due at Myghelmas the yere abouesaid	xxiij li xij s viij d

[Marginal note]
Here begynnyth the Chargys for the Remouyng doune of ye Com[m]unyon tabyll and allso For the quere wyth the makyng of pewys w[i]th other charg[es]

It[e]m to Wyllyam Trewe and his man for vij th dayes worke	xj s viij d
It[e]m for CCC di[midium] [350] of borde	xvij s vj d
It[e]m to ij laborers at vij d the daye	xiiij d
It[e]m for ij punityons and a quarter	xiij d
It[e]m to a Joyno[u]^r for iiij dayes at xij d ye daie	iiij s

3 Instructions for watching and firing beacons and aiding the Navy, 1596

After my hartye Commendations unto you, My Lorde Admirall Wilbe

at Rochester or Chatham a tuesdaye nexte, praie therfore do you attende •
his Lo[rdship] where he shall then be that you maie understand by him
what coarses his Lo[rdship] shall thinke fitt to be taken for the better
securitye of her Ma[jes]ties NAVYE, the w[hi]ch you must have speciall
care to see performed and I also praie you to write your l[ett]res to the
Justic[es] of everye devic[i]on to see that the Beacons be well and
stronglye watched by men of discrec[i]on. My Lo[rde] and I, am of
opinion that the maner of the Beacon[es] should in this be altered, that
whereas men are to goe upp as it were by a Lather to fyer the Barrel[es]
the same should be lett downe and upp by a rope w[i]th a pullee: for
that yf the wynde should be highe, yt would be fearfull to many to goe
upp, what neede soever required to have the Beacon fyered wherein as
his Lo[rdship] shall take order, as also for any newe watche or garde
praye see yt done accordinglye, And lastlye that the Companies appointed for the succor of the NAVIE, and for the Isle of Shepie maie be
commaunded to be in a readines at all tymes to performe the same:
And so I Committ you to god, From the Cowrte at Ritchemond this
first of November 1596.

I marveile that I heare
not from you of the receipte   Your lovinge freinde
of my former Letters   Cobham
To my Lovinge freindes S[i]r Jhon Levesonne Knighte
and Mr. Thomas Walsingha[m] esquier my Deputie Lieuetenaunt[es]

4 (a) Archbishop Laud's visitation of diocese of Lichfield, 1635

Marchington.   Noe p[er]ambulation, a disorder in the Chauncell by the
servant[es] of the p[ar]ishion[er]s (though warned to
sitt in another place appointed for them).
Thomas Cooke for not standinge up att the Creed.
Rob[er]tus Moreton vt sup[r]ᵃ [as above].

nil $\left\{ \begin{array}{l} \text{(Elizabetha Gilbert} \\ \text{(Dorothea Dixon} \end{array} \right.$ midwives whether licensed or noe
wee knowe not comp[arui]ᵗ
[appeared].

Predictus [the aforesaid] Thomas Cooke, not duly
cominge to Evening prayer, but goes to another Church.
Ed[uard]us Poole gen[erosus] et ⎫ pro Recusan[tia]
eius ux[or]   ⎬ et absen[tia]
Nich[ola]us Deykin & Anna eius ⎭ ab Eccl[es]ia
ux[or]

[Edward Poole gentleman and his wife and Nicholas Deykin and Anne his wife, for recusancy and absence from church.]

4 (b) Bishop's visitation of diocese of Chichester, 1636

Richardus Randall et Jo[hannes] Westbrooke gard[iani] ib[ide]m p[er]sonal[ite]r Citat[i] p[er] eundem eodem die pro ca[us]a sequen[ti] vi[delicet]

[Richard Randall and John Westbrooke [church] wardens there cited by the same on the same day for the following cause]

Elsted The Church want[es] shingling in many places.

There want[es] a new Pulpett, That w[hi]^{ch} is there already is too lowe & not uniforme.

Purific- The Seat[es] in the Chauncell are much decayed.

ac[i]o[n]is The Church want[es] to be beautified w[i]th Sentences of

xx^d Scripture.

The Ten Comaundem[en]^{ts} & the King[es] Armes which are sett up in the Church are very dymm & almost worne out.

The Churchyard is not kept sweet & cleane but is full of rubbish.

There is neither Cloth nor Cushion for the Pulpett.

They have not the Service Booke for the 5th of November.

5 (a) Archbishop's visitation book, 1595

[Manchester]

They presente one Jackeson for teachinge a Schole, in Mr Will[ia]m Hollandes house, not lycensed.

John Tonge practyseth phisicke, not lycensed.

5 (b) Testimonial by 28 Whitby men on behalf of a Schoolmaster, 1679

Wee whose names are heerunto subscribed beeing Inhabitants of the Towne and p[ar]ish of Whitby doe humbly certifie That whereas wee are informed, some p[er]sonns have Cast an aspersion upon Mr Christopher Stephenson on whose behalfe wee formerly Certified, desireing that hee might have a license to teach schoole in Whitby, that hee is a Nonconformist a Consorter with quakers and phanaticks, which was an obstruction to his proceedings in that good way of educatinge children, which wee know to be false and a scandall upon him, for that wee have seen him a constant Church man both in Whitby, and att Fylingdales ever since his Coming to this p[ar]te of the Countrie, and noe consorter with phanaticks otherwise then all others doe in ordinary Com[m]unicac[i]on and to this wee sett our hands the 4 Aug[ust] 1679.

6 (a) Warrant by the Lord Mayor of London for fire-fighting, 1642

To the Aldram[en] of the
Ward of Bridge w[i]thout   By the Maior
For the better Prevenc[i]on & secureing of this Citty from the danger of fire w[hi]^{ch} in these Turbulent & disastrous tymes may be attempted (amongst other practises against the same) by those whoe are Enemies to the peace and saftey thereof These are earnestley to requier & com[m]aund you your deputie & Com[m]on Counsell men of yo[u]^r Ward to cause the Engine (if any be) p[ro]vided for the quenching of Fire) within yo[u]^r ward to be imediatly without all delay p[re]pared and fitted for vse And if your Ward be yet unprovided thereof then to take the speediest course you possibly may to supply the want of this Instrument soe vsefull & necessary to the securing of this Citty & how ye are p[ro]vided & what ye shall doe herein to make retorne vnto me within 24 hower next after the receit hereof Alsoe these are to requier you to call hefore you the Churchwardens of every of your severall p[ar]ishes within your ward & strictley to inioyne them with all possible hast & speed to provide for theire owne parishes respectiueley strong & sufficient Ladders hoockes & Bucketts with twoe pick-hatchet[es] . . .

6 (b) Note by the Clerk of the Peace for Nottinghamshire, 1642

Here the Warres between the King & Parliam[en]^t begun
and interrupted all legall proceeding[es].

7 Sequestration of the Cornish estate of the Earl of Salisbury, 1642

Wheras the Earle of Salisbury holds the Mannor of Trerabo, and the Sheafes of S[ain]^t Illary & Clements in Cornwall (sometime belonging

to S[ain]ᵗ Michaells Mount, now the Inheritance of Francis Bassett
Esq[uire]) of the Crowne, by which he is bound to serue his Ma[jes]ᵗⁱᵉ
in his Warres, Whiche he hath not onlie Neglected to doe, but hath still
Adhered to his Ma[jes]ᵗⁱᵉˢ Enemies, by giving his Vote with Them,
in their Treason. And wheras Wee his Ma[jes]ᵗⁱᵉˢ Com[m]issioners to
command in chief in the West, haue given Command & Authority to
You Francis Bassett Esq[uire] To Your very great Charge to fortifie
& keep a Garrison in the said S[ain]t Michaells Mount being a Place of
very great strength, & of much Importance for the safetie of this
Countie, & very vsefull to his Ma[jes]ᵗⁱᵉˢ service, Wee doe therfore
thinke fitt, & Order that the said Mannor, & Sheafes be againe Annexed
to the said Mount. And to that End Wee doe hereby Authorize you to
seize & take into Yo[u]r hands the said Mannor of Trerabo, & Sheafes,
with the Rents, & Command all the Tenants of the said Mannor &
Sheafes to pay their Rents Unto You: And such as you shall Assigne,
And all Whome this Concernes, are to take Notice herof, & to giue
Obedience vnto the same. And for soe doeing, This shallbe to You,
& Them a Sufficient Warrant. Dated 1ʳ of December. 1642.

> Warwicke Mohun
> Ralph Hopton
> John Berkeley

9 (a) Quarter Sessions, Bedfordshire, 1658

Bed[fordshire] At the Generall Quarter Sessions of the publick Peace
holden for the County of Bedford at the Towne of Bedford in the said
Countie on Munday next after the close of Easter being the xix th day
of Aprill in the Yeare of our Lord 1658

2. Indictm[en]t ag[ains]t William Athey of Harrold Butcher for that
   being Constable he spake these word[es], I care not a fart for any
   Justice of the peace in England.

   > App[er]es & imp[ar]les confesses fine xij p[ai]d
   > discharged

2. Indictm[en]t ag[ains]t Daniel Knight of Luton Taylor for a battery
   upon Robert Cooper.

   > Submitt[es] w[i]th p[ro]test[?ation] fine xij d.

[78]

10 (a) Ordinance, Bristol Common Council, against soapmakers, 1566

M[emoran]d[um] that whereas before this tyme great inconvenyence and detryment hath rysen and growen by casting of Sopers asshes into the Ryver of this Citie at sundry places by certen p[er]sons of the crafte of Sopemakers, whereby many bankes and quarres by growen in the said River, w[hi]che in shorte tyme (if spedye remedye be not provided) is like to redowne to the vtter decaie and destrucc[i]on of the same River. It is nowe therefore ordayned for reformac[i]on thereof by the w[o]rshipfull John Cutt Maior the Aldremen Shriff[es] and others of the com[m]on Councaill of the citie of Bristowe whose names be hereafter written that noe p[er]son or p[er]sons of the said crafte of Sopemakers, nor any other, shall at any tyme hereafter convey or carie by water or caste or laie, or cause to be caried caste or laied any sope asshes either in the said River, or any p[ar]te thereof, or . . .

10 (b) Licence to collect for relief of flood victims, Bristol, 1673-4

By the Mayor & Ald[er]m[en] the 20th of
January 1673 [1674]

Civitas You are forthwith desired Im[m]ediately on sight hereof to
goe from Doore to Doore w[i]thin yo[u]r p[ar]ish & to
Bristoll receaue the Charrity of well disposed people towarde the
speedy releife of such poore p[er]sons & families in the
p[ar]ish of S[ain]t James, that are in very great Extremity &
want, through the late Inundation & Overflowing of the
Waters, And ye monies you shall soe Collect to bring to
Mr Mayor who will take Care that ye same be Justly disposed
of, to those necessitous p[er]sons as afores[ai]d.

Temple   Ric[har]d Streamer May[o]r
To Mr Tippett &   Jo[h]n Lawford
Mr Rogers   Ralph Olliffe

11 (a) Depositions against George Fox referred to Lancashire J.P.s, 1652

To y[e] Justices of Peace for y[e] Hundred of Loynsedall
with in y[e] Countie of Lancaster:

Wee thought good to signifie to your Wor[shi]pps y[t] [that] one George Foxe hath beene lately in these parts and hath uttered seuerall blasphemies w[hi]ch are unfitting to bee mentioned and therefore our desire is y[t] you would bee pleased to heare what seuerall witnesses can attest

[79]

against him and so proceede with this offend[e]ʳ as yᵉ Law in such case hath prouided, and wee shall bee perpetually oblidged to you:/ [signatures of five witnesses].

[The remainder of the document is not illustrated]

Wee thought good to give you a narrative of such things as will bee made out against him:

1. He did affirme that he had the divinitie essentially in him.
2. That both baptisme and the Lords Supper were unlawful.
3. He did dissuade men from readinge the scripture tellinge them that it was carnall.   Michaell Altham sworne.
1. That he was equall with God.
2. That God taught deceit.
3. That Scriptures were Antichrist.
4. That he was the Judge of the world.
5. That he was as upright as Christ.

William Smyth, Nathanael Atkinson, sworne.

Taken in open sessions at Lancaster 5 October 1652 before us
Geo: Toulnson, John Sawrey [J.P.s].
Make 2 warrants against him [note by Clerk of the Peace].

11 (b) Three Warwickshire J.P.s asked to arrange for repair of Alveston Bridge on the Avon, 1658

Warwickes[hire] At the generall Sessions of the publiq[ue] peace holden at Warwicke in and for the County aforesaid upon Tuesday

Easter next after the close of the feast of East[e]ʳ that is to say the
1658 twentieth day of Aprill in the yeare of our Lord one thousand six hundred fifty and eight.

Whereas this Court was this day informed, on the behalfe of divers of the Inhabitants of this County, that Alveston Bridge lying over the river of Avon is much fallen into decay and in want of repaire, Whereupon it was desired that some effectuall course might be taken in order to the repaire thereof: It is therefore

Alves- thought fitt and ordered that Richard Lucy esq[ui]ʳ[e] Colonel
ton Hawksworth and Major Bridges or any two of them shalbe
bridge and are hereby desired to take a view of the said bridge, and to consider who ought to repaire the same, and what the charge thereof will be, and to treate with honest workemen for the said repaires, and to certifie their doings and opinions

[80]

(a) Deposition, 1598, at Guildford Borough Court by a Surrey coroner about 'creckett' and 'baytinge of beares' fifty years earlier when he was at Guildford Free-School. (Believed to be the earliest known mention of cricket.) (*Transcript* on p. 73.)

1. Cricket and Football

(b) Presentment at Essex Quarter Sessions of ten men for playing on Sunday 'at an unlawfull game called the fote bale wheron grew bludshedd', 1599. (*Transcript* on p. 74.)

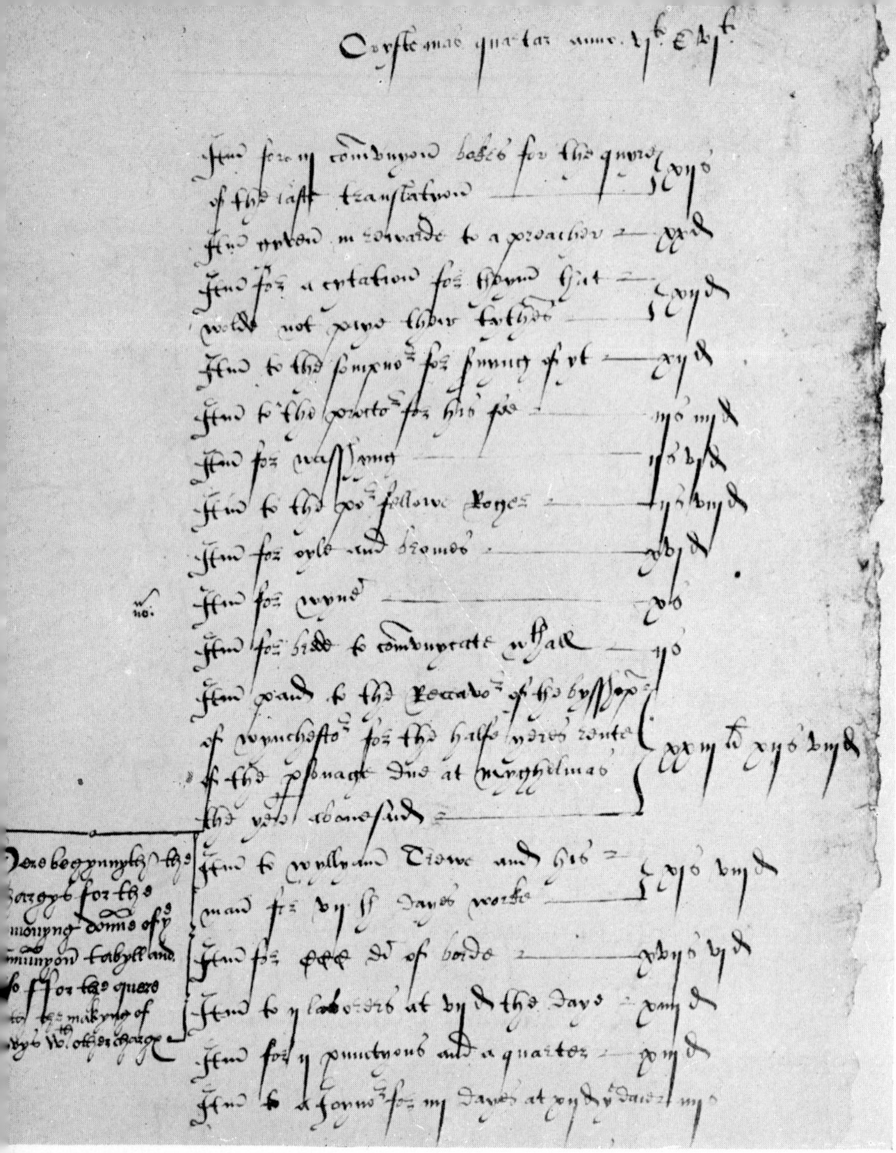

2. Church Account and Poor Rate, Parish of St. Saviour, Southwark

(a) Churchwardens' expenses, Christmas quarter, 6 Edward VI, 1552–53. The first entry and the marginal note refer to the furthest limits of the Protestant government's liturgical changes; the revised edition of the Prayer Book had just come into use. St. Saviour's church, now Southwark cathedral, was an Augustinian priory until the Dissolution. (*Transcript* on p. 74; for Queen Mary's restoration of the Mass, see *Extracts*, 1, p. 84.)

(b) One entry in the rate-list of the overseers of the poor, 1621, marking each of 52 weekly payments of 3d. (hence no 'arrears') by Thomas Harverd (brother of John, founder of Harvard College [later University], 1638, baptized here when his father was a churchwarden .

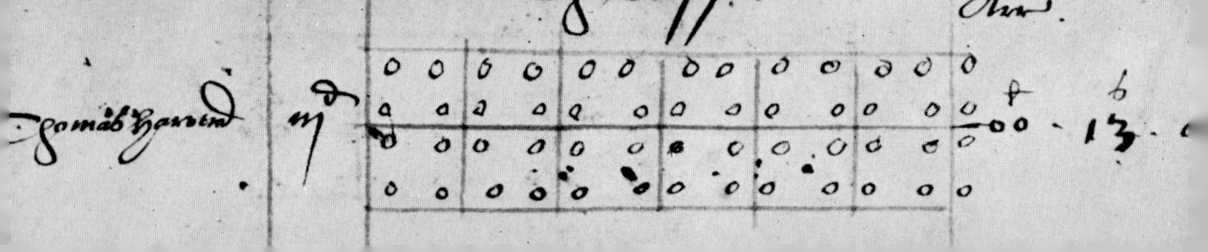

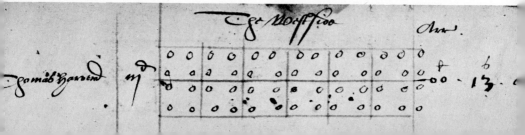

3. Invasion Beacons

Lord Cobham, Lieutenant of the county of Kent, gives his Deputy Lieutenants instructions to pass to J.P.s for watching and firing beacons and aiding the Navy, 1596. (*Transcript* on p. 74.)

(a) Archbishop Laud's visitation of the diocese of Lichfield:
parish of Marchington, Staffordshire, 1635. (*Transcript* on p. 75.)

4. Church Visitations

Periodic tours of inspection by the bishops and less often by the archbishops or their deputies revealed defects in churches and delinquencies among parishioners.

(b) Bishop's visitation of diocese of Chichester:
parish of Elsted, Sussex, 1636. (*Transcript* on p. 76.)

(a) Archbishop's visitation book, 1595. Presentments for teaching and for practising medicine without licence, Manchester. (Transcript on p. 76.)

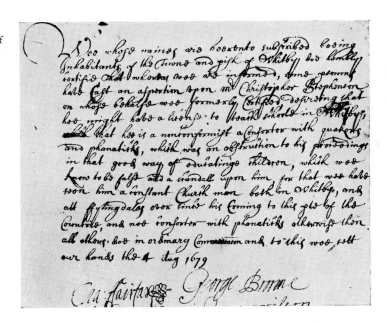

(b) Testimonial by Whitby men on behalf of a school-teacher, 1679. (Transcript on p. 76.)

(c) Plan attached to faculty granted by Archbishop for new church, Kinoulton, Notts., 1792. (See p. 43.)

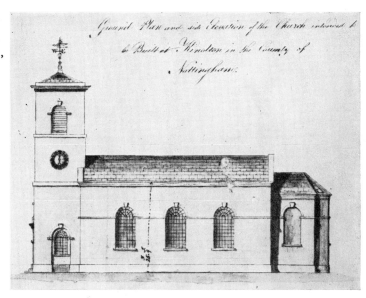

5. Church Licensing—Province of York

6. Civil War (1)

(a) One of the precepts issued by the Lord Mayor of London to City parishes and wards for getting fire engines and equipment ready 'in these turbulent and disastrous tymes', 1642. (*Transcript* on p. 77.)

(b) Note by the Clerk of the Peace for Nottinghamshire, 1642.

7. Civil War (2)

Order by the Royalists for sequestration of the Cornish estate
of the Earl of Salisbury, a Parliamentarian, the income to be
used for defence of St. Michael's Mount, 1642. (*Transcript* on p. 77.)

City of Glouc[ester]

Ordinances Statutes and Rules made and ordained by the Maior Aldermen and Common Counsell of this City of Gloucester, at a Counsell holden in their Counsell Chamber the Seaventeenth day of November in the yeare of our Lord God One Thousand Six hundred ffifty and three according to the computation of the Church of England, for the good Government of the severall Hospitalls of St Bartholmew, King James Hospitall, and the Hospitall of St Margaret, all in the Governance and disposing of the Maior and Burgesses of this City, and for the guiding and ordering of the poore people in the said Hospitalls. And allso for the direction of the Governors there appointed in their severall Offices and places under the paines and penalties herein lymitted and according to the manner and forme hereafter following.

First it is ordered and enacted that there shalbe yearely Eight officers or Governors of the said Hospitalls chosen, to wit a President a Treasurer, two Surveyors, two Almoners, and two Stewards.

8. Hospitals for the Poor

(a) Ordinances made by Gloucester Corporation for the City hospitals, 1653. Hospitals were originally for the destitute, aged and infirm.

(b) One of Chester's many charters, 1658. Oliver Cromwell (portrait inside 'O') grants to the City the care of the ancient Hospital of St. John the Baptist. (See p. 35.)

(a) Quarter Sessions, Bedfordshire, 1658. (*Transcript* on p. 78.)

9. Quarter and Petty Sessions

The Quarter Sessions rolls or order books for many counties have been printed for varying periods, but early Petty Sessions records are relatively rare. (See pp. 23 and 31.)

(b) Sutton-at-Hone Petty Sessions, Kent, 1709.

(a) Ordinance of Bristol Common Council
against the soapmakers, 1566. (*Transcript* on p. 79).

10. River and Flood

(b) Licence to collect money for relief of
flood victims, Bristol, 1673–74 (pasted into vestry minute book
of Temple parish, Bristol). (*Transcript* on p. 79.)

(a) Allegations against George Fox referred
to Lancashire J.P.s, 1652. (*Transcript*, with further details, on p. 79.)

11. J.P.s' Judicial and Administrative Duties

(b) Richard Lucy and two other Warwickshire J.P.s
asked to arrange for repair of
Alveston Bridge on the Avon, 1658. (*Transcript* on p. 80.)

(a) Accounts of ironworks on Cannock Chase, Staffordshire, 1578.
These ironworks included the first known blast furnace in the Midlands. (*Transcript* on p. 81.)

12. Iron and Coal

(b) Agreement between two Monmouthshire men to
'open coaleworks and myneworks', sharing profits equally, 1684.

(a) Sacrament certificate given to a Hertfordshire squire by minister and churchwardens, 1703.

WE Robert Whitehead + + + Minister of the Parish
Parish-Church of Greate Gaddesden in ye County of Her
and John Crokett + Church-Warden of the same Parish
Parish-Church, do hereby Certifie, That Thomas Halsey of the
and County aforesayd Esq; + + + + + +

+ + + + + + + + upon the Lord's Day, commonly ca
Sunday, the Twenty Eighth + ++ Day of March 1703 + + in
diately after Divine Service and Sermon, did in the Parish-Church afore
receive the Sacrament of the Lord's Supper, according to the custom of the Ch
of England. In Witness whereof, We have hereunto Subscribed our H
the sayd Twenty Eighth + Day of March + + + in the Ye
our Lord, One Thousand Seven Hundred and three.

Robert Whitehead. Minister of the Parish
Parish-Church of Greate Gaddesden in Co
Church Warden of the
Parish and Parish-Ch

the mark of
John O Crokett

Leonard Bowles of the p^rish of Greate Gaddesden in
County of Hertford and Joh. Webb of ye same +
do severally make Oath, That they do know Thomas Halsey Esqr
in the above-written Certificate named, and who now present hath delivere
same into this Court: And do further severally make Oath, that they di
the said Thomas Halsey + receive the Sacrament of the Lord's Su
in the Parish Church of Greate Gaddesden + + +
+ + in the said Certificate, mentioned; and upon the Day, and at the ti
the said Certificate, in that behalf certified and expressed: And that they d
the Certificate above-written, Subscribed by the said Robert Whiteh
and John Crokett + + + + + + + And further the
Leonard Bowles and John Webb + + + do say upon their respe
Oaths, That all other Matters or Things in the said Certificate recited, ment
or expressed, are true as they verily believe. Leonard Bowles

the mark of
John X Webb.

(b) Minutes of Quarterly Meeting of Society of Friends for counties of Salop, Montgomery and Merioneth, granting money to Quakers going to Pennsylvania, 1690.

Meeting
Dolobran,
29th: 5: month
1690

And as to what was formerly proposed to this meeting
about helping a poor Friend called Robert Ellis with
his wife and Children towards Pensylvania from Penlly
Salop and Mountgomery sh. Friends concluded to send
each of them 50 shillings in all 5^lb which is desired to be
sent before the 25^t of the next month to Bala And
Merioneth sh. friends purpose to make it up 15^lb
by raysing 10^lb more in their County. If the man do not
... the money is to be retained

(a) Bristol Corporation apprenticeship book, 1626.
A sailor's son apprenticed to a carpenter (he was ship's carpenter on the *Mayflower*), who
covenants to convey to the youth 25 acres in New England and 15 bushels of wheat. (*Transcript* on p. 81.)

14. Emigrants and Negroes

Bristol and Liverpool records tell much about those who left England
to people the New World and those who engaged in the slave trade.

(b) Indentured
servants sailing
to Virginia in the
Concord, 1698
(first few
entries). Names
of apprenticed
servants with
captains and
ships sailing from
Liverpool were
kept by the
Town Clerk.

(c) Account ren-
dered to a Liver-
pool merchant
for sale of slaves
transported from
Africa in the
Lottery, 1798.

Appointment by [Ric]hard Lord [Prot]ector of the [She]riff of Norfolk, [165]8, with [Gre]at Seal of [the] Commonwealth. ([Tr]anscript on p. 82.)

15. Sheriff and Lieutenant

The Saxon shire-reeve, who became a very powerful officer in medieval times, was responsible to the King for the gaol, the execution of the laws and the collection of the Crown revenues in each country. The Tudors entrusted his military functions to a new county officer, the King's Lieutenant, who in turn appointed Deputy Lieutenants; they were actively engaged in military matters until the 1745 Rebellion and again in 1796–1805 when the French threatened invasion. See p. 32. Lieutenancy documents, usually of much interest (see Plate 3), occur in official county records and in private archives.

Appointment by [the] Earl of Malton, [Lor]d Lieutenant of [the] West Riding of [Yor]kshire, of Earl [Fit]zwilliam as a [De]puty Lieutenant, [174]4.

(a) Accounts of coal sold and delivered at Leeds Staithe (Wharf) from Middleton Colliery, 1764.

(b) Kirkstall (Leeds) Forge accounts, 1811.
This Company claims to be continuing the iron manufacture at the Kirkstall forge of the Cistercian abbey.

(c) Middleton Colliery working expenses, 1814.

VILTS, *to wit.* } THE General Quarter Sessions of the Peace of our Lord the King, held at *New Sarum,* in and for the said County of *Wilts,* on *Tuesday* the *twenty sixth* Day of *April* in the *Forty eighth* Year of the Reign of our Sovereign Lord GEORGE the Third, by the Grace of God of the United Kingdom of *Great Britain* and *Ireland,* King, Defender of the Faith, before *the Right Honorable the Earl of Radnor, John Henry Jacob Clerk*

and Others, their Fellows, Justices of our said Lord the King, assigned to keep the Peace of the said King, in the County aforesaid ; and also to hear and determine divers Felonies, Trespasses, and other Misdemeanors, done and committed in the said County.

THIS COURT doth choose and appoint *William Burgess of Westbury* in the said County of *Wilts,* to be one of the INSPECTORS of the Mills, Shops, Outhouses, and Tentor Grounds of the Clothiers, Millmen, and other Persons concerned in the manufacturing and milling of MIXED or MEDLEY WOOLLEN BROAD CLOTH within the said County of *Wilts,* until the General Quarter Sessions of the Peace to be holden in and for the said County next after *Easter,* pursuant to the Act of Parliament passed in the Thirteenth Year of the Reign of His late Majesty King GEORGE the First.

An Extract of the Act of Parliament

Made and passed in the Thirteenth Year of the Reign of His late Majesty King GEORGE the First, relating to the

DUTY OF INSPECTORS
OF MIXED OR MEDLEY WOOLLEN BROAD CLOTH.

SECTION X.

AND BE IT FURTHER ENACTED, by the Authority aforesaid, That for preventing the ill-Practices used in the excessive straining of Mixed or Medley Woollen Broad Cloth, every Owner or Proprietor of Tentor or Tentors, Rack or Racks, for such Cloth, within the Counties of *Gloucester, Wilts,* and *Somerset,* shall, after the first Day of August, one thousand even hundred and twenty-seven, and he is hereby required to measure such Tentor or Tentors,

(a) Appointment by Wiltshire Quarter Sessions of cloth inspector, 1809.

17. West Country Cloth

Day for Whippisley's late Webb's — D: — 2 2
D: for two new Houses in S. Street — D: — 3 —
D: for Tenem:ts in Howtry — D: — 1 —
Mn Lewis for pt of Leader Hyatt's D: — — 4
D: for a new House — D: — — 0.
Sundries for Stock in Trade
Mr Westley Clothier for — £210 . 15 — 10 11¼
D:o as Cloth worker — 40 . . — 2 .
210 . 15 — 10 11¼

(b) Extract from a Somerset parish poor rate-book, 1793 ('clothier' meant clothmaker.) (See p. 54.)

(For Select Vestry, see p. 56.)

Leyton Workhouse, 1st Octr 1821.

At a Special Meeting of the Select Vestry, holden this Day.

Mr Richardson laid before the Vestry an Order, under the Seals of 2 Magistrates, dated the 29th Ultimo, for the Removal [of] Bathsheba Pollard, Single woman, with Child, from this Parish [to] the Parish of St James Clerkenwell, Middlesex.

Ordered — That the Order of Magistrates be carried into Execution with little delay as possible.

18. The Poor

(a) Leyton, Essex, deals with an unmarried mother, 1821.
(For Select Vestry, see p. 56.)

(b) A Yorkshire pauper writes to overseers of his home parish near Wakefield, 1827. (See p. 60.)

(c) The Master of Oswestry Union Workhouse, Salop, punishes two inmates, 1860. (For Boards of Guardians, see p. 33.)

Skipton January 5. 1827
Sir
I write those few lines to inform you that I have got [no work]
Nor cannot hear of any and that I have no shoes or
have come over myself our landlord has been for the
Remainder of the Rent and if it is not paid very soon
he will make A distress and sell what we have
I thought of going into Lancashire to seek work but
have no shoes nor money to go with besides my wife
Child has nothing to take to
the bearer will testify of the Situation we are in
William Thompson

No. of Case	NAME.	OFFENCE.	Date of Offence.	Punishment inflicted by Master or other Officer
79	Wm Williams	Insolent to the Master	1860 Jan 6	Brought before the [Board] Reprimanded —
80	Wm Williams	Reporting in Town that the thickest & best of the gruel was given to the pigs instead of the Paupers	Dec 31	Stopped his leave & Tobacco till brought before the Board

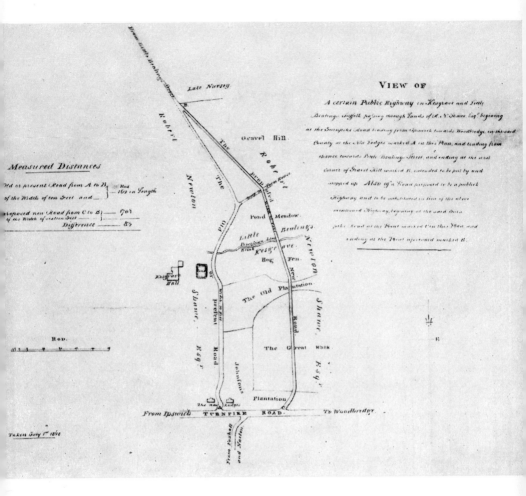

19. Diversion of a Highway

Proposed new road at Kesgrave Hall, Suffolk, 1828.
Two or more J.P.s had power to close unnecessary roads and footpaths
or to divert them subject to there being no appeal to Quarter Sessions.
This typical map shows a diversion designed to increase the area of a
park and the owner's privacy. (See p. 27.)

20. Iron Railroads

Two items from the archives of Dowlais Iron Company (now absorbed into Guest, Keen & Co.) (See p. 70.)

(a) Specification for rails, Liverpool and Manchester Railway, 1836

(b) Letter from the directors of a Russian railroad company, 1836.

Ap.r 29.	20 y.d fine Crimson Velvet	26.	26: 0: 0
	8 y.d Crimson Mantua	7.	2: 16: 0
	14 y.d Crimson Sasnet	2:6.	1: 15: 0
	19 ½ y.d white brocaded Sultane	21.	20: 9: 6
	8 y.d white Italian Lutestring	6:6.	2: 12: 0
	14 y.d white Sasnet	2:6.	1: 15: 0
	Two boxes.		0: 3: 0
Nov.r 14.	15 y.d pink brocaded double Ground	20.	15: 0

(a) Bill for rich fabrics bought in London by a Bristol man, 1729.

21. Personal Accounts

(See p. 67.)

(b) Accounts of a Worcestershire woman, 1743.

1743

June y.e 25.th for two Knotts & Breastknotts	00	03	00
Aug.st y.e 29.th then paid for two pair of Stockings	00	09	00
Sep.r y.e 10.th then bought a Silk Handkerchief	00	04	00
y.e 12.th then paid M.rs Wheeler	11	10	00
with evend all accompts between her & me.			
y.e Same Day for two Necklesses	00	02	00
Curling Irons	00	02	00
two pair of Gloves	00	02	08
for painting y.e Coat of Armes on y.e Chair			
& a New Steep	00	10	00
for Dryd Sweetmeats	00	11	00
Oct. y.e 5.th for two pair of Childrens Gloves & one			
for my Self	00	03	05
y.e 9.th then evend all accompts with Tho: Winn			
Nov.r y.e 6 then paid M.r Blayney 10. 13 & evend all			
accompts with him			
y.e Same day for 5 ½ y.ds of riband			
	00	03	06

(a) Final Concord (or Fine), 1580, between Wm. Deynes and Tho. Goodriche gentlemen (plaintiffs) and Wm. Goodriche and wife Eliz. (deforciants). A messuage, a garden, 16 acres arable, 5 ac. meadow and 60 ac. pasture in five Suffolk parishes.

22. Manuscripts in Miniature: (1) Two documents of title

Many bundles of deeds include either or both of these strange-looking documents recording fictitious suits in the Royal Courts and contrived in order to register title or to bar the entail, the wife's dower or all contingent remainders (see p. 67). Most can be easily recognised, the Fine by its two wavy edges and opening phrase, 'Hec est finalis Concordia . . .' (This is the final Agreement), the Recovery by the royal portrait inside initial letter, the county followed by two parties' names linked by 'petit versus' (sues against) in the third or fourth line, by the narrow archaic writing, and by the appended court seal in a round tin case.

(b) Common Recovery, 1728. Dan. Vickers against Jos. Cole, gentlemen. 3 messuages, 2 gardens, 12 ac. arable, 10 ac. meadow and 30 ac. pasture in two Suffolk parishes. 1st vouchee, Peter Clayton; 2nd vouchee, Jas. Morland.

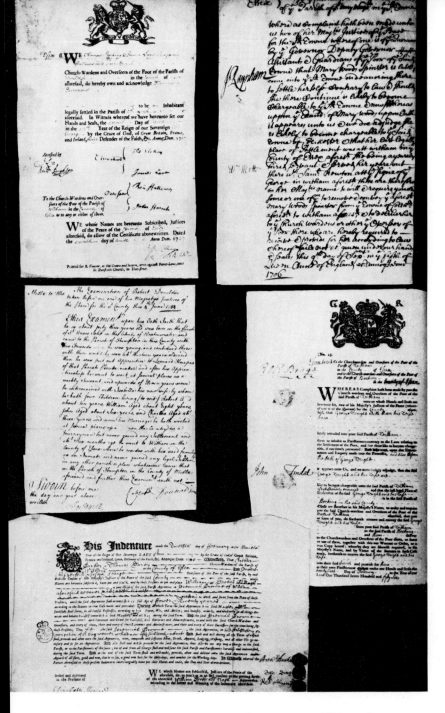

23. Manuscripts in Miniature: (2) Settlement papers, Witham, Essex

For many parishes hundreds of these papers have survived. (See p. 60.)

(a) Indemnity certificate, 1727.
(c) Examination, 1744.
(e) Apprenticeship indenture, 1711.

(b) Removal order to Witham, 1706.
(d) Removal order from Witham, 1756.

24. Water and Fire

(a) Expense accounts of the Bedford Level, properly called the Great Level of the Fens, 1663–64.

The Great Level (165,000 acres) was divided into North, Middle and South Levels: accounts relate to the last – the Great Ouse in Cambridgeshire and the tributaries from Suffolk and Norfolk. The endless struggle against the combined forces of tidal and river flooding elsewhere is chronicled in the Commissioners of Sewers records (see p. 32.)

(b) London Fire Brigade daily fire reports, 1861. Third entry records the outbreak of the Great Fire of Tooley Street and [last column] the death of the Superintendent of the Fire Engine Establishment. Entries about this event run into five pages.

25. Letters from Oxford and Cambridge Undergraduates

(a) Edmund Verney, Magdalen, Oxford, to his brother at Claydon, Bucks., 1636.

(b) Edward 4th Viscount Irwin, Christ's, Cambridge, to his steward at Temple Newsam near Leeds, 1703.

Ser
I have Trobbulyou with thee fuu Lins
Consaun this horred afer with i ham in
oxon Casel for oral Last With is Laid to
My Charge Ther is no douct Ser you
bin at a dal of Trobel a bot it &
a dael of exspenc bot Sr villabe hou
happey tis for me to go to this on timle
fnd Vich i exspaks in a short tim
and to bol god to be a Vitness of hee to
deniit for me Vich i Can Vich a Saftee
Gonshonsh i thank god for it
Ther is no doct bot the poor man Lot is Lifte
Bab Ser villabe it not fond out it
and fou you old find Vend tis to Late for
me bot bot it onlley Ser Taking my Life
Ther is the poor Vidder that Vill bee Left to
goo and the Vide Vorld and my Poor mother
and Feather Vith sorow to ther Graves bot the
hoat to make ther selfe happey mor so
Then if I had bin Giltley of it with I han
Not I think god I ~~~~ I ~~~~
I hope you and your Famley Vill Live to
Fiind that Giles Freeman Covington did
hinhersent and Then I hop you old releve
the Vidder that Left bind if beedlum
is not her dom in flts of fulline my
Life bin gon Vich Vill be of no servis
So no mar at ~~present~~ from ~~you it~~
the unfortnet youth Giles Freeman.
I hope god Will bee Vith Covington
you and yours

26. Letter from a Condemned Murderer

Covington, prisoner in the condemned cell at Oxford Castle Gaol, 1791, protests his
innocence to Christopher Willoughby, J.P., who committed him for trial for
murdering a Scots pedlar in 1787. A few days later he was hanged, and his body
handed over to the University School of Anatomy for dissection. For the next
150 years his skeleton was used to illustrate the skeletal anatomy of 'an
Englishman' and it now rests in the Bone Room of the Department of Zoology
and Comparative Anatomy. (Found in the Willoughby family archives.)

27. Parish Register and Bishop's Transcript

(a) Register of St. Cuthbert, Bedford, 1672–73.
'Dafter' (daughter) and other colloquial forms suggest that the scribe was the parish clerk. The fourth baptism has been interlined in a literate, contemporary hand: it does not occur in the B.T.; see (b). Is 'John Bunyan' the author of *The Pilgrim's Progress* or his son? There is conflicting evidence of his identity.
(*Transcript* on p. 82.)

(b) Bishop's transcript, Broughton Hackett, Worcs., 1683–84.
Each year after Easter the churchwardens were obliged to send a transcript of the register entries for the preceding year to the bishop's (or archdeacon's) registrar. Those surviving may be invaluable in several ways (see p. 42).
(*Transcript* on p. 82.)

28. Private Estate Maps

(a) Map of town of Petworth, Sussex, *circa* 1630, Surveyor adopts the bird's-eye method with advantage, but his draughtsmanship is not equal to that in *Plate* 29.

(b) Map of one of the Open Fields of Church Aston, Shropshire, 1681, showing intermixed strips of various owners. 'Cop', copyhold. 'Key' is a surname.

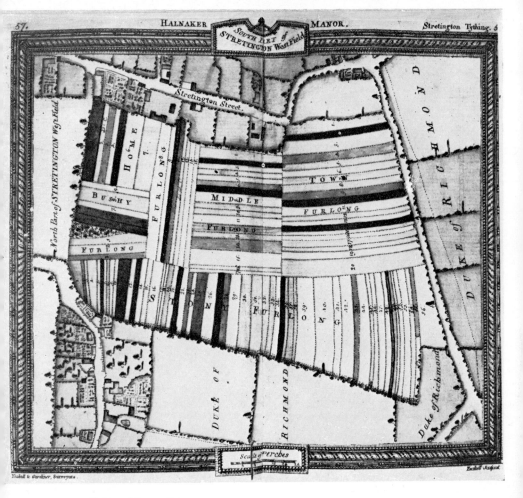

29. Private Estate Map

One of a series of maps of Strettington, Sussex, 1781, showing village street and strips in several furlongs of one of the open fields. Note the fine details. The frame is not real, but drawn in. Maps for rich landowners often reveal surveyors' exquisite draughtsmanship.

30. Private Estate Map

Part of Map of Clayworth, Nottinghamshire, 1749. Shows the open (common) fields, with hundreds of narrow strips, also some partial enclosure. Clayworth Common is in top right-hand corner.

Private estate maps were often embellished with the owner's coat-of-arms and occasionally with a drawing of the mansion (as here) and with an elaborate cartouche, compass-rose and scale.

31. Greens and Tithes

(a) Enclosure Award map of two Lancashire commons, 1751. (See p. 25.)

(b) Small part of Tithe Apportionment (or Award) map of Wateringbury, Kent, 1841, showing village street and land use including orchards and hopfields. (See p. 41.)

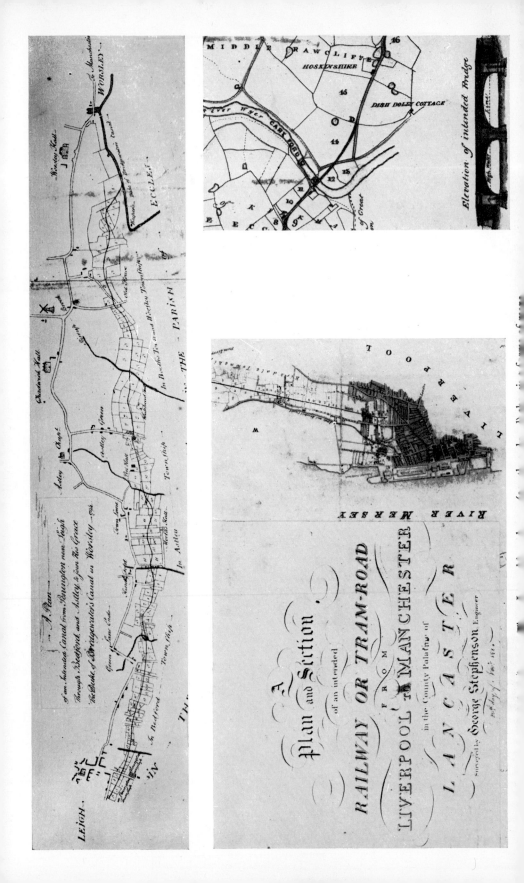

therein to the next gen[er]all Sessions of the peace to be held for this County, to the end the said Bridge may be repaired accordingly.

12 (a) Accounts of ironworks on Cannock Chase, Staffordshire, 1578

viij Novembris 1578   Payment[es] in Tedesley

To Lawrance Angell for colinge –

Collyar[es] in	of xv lod[es] of coles	xxij^s vj^d
Tedesley	Milling[es] for – xvij lod[es]	xxv^s vj^d
	Aberleye – xiiij lod[es]	xxj^s
Caryage	To Mr Lyttleton for caringe of xxxv	
of Coles	lod[es] of coles	xxiij^s iiij^d
	To John Symons for ij Found[eres] –	xxiiij^s
	for makinge his harth & dressinge the	xj^s
	Bellas	
Founder[es]	to him in reward for makinge y^e	x^s
	Newe Fornes	

14 (a) Apprenticeship register, Bristol, 1626

Quarto die decembre[is] [4 Dec.]

Franciscus	Johannes Morgan filius Ed[ua]r[d]i Morgan nup[er]
Eaton	de Ciui[ta]te Bristoll sailer def[uncti] posuit se app
	[re]ntic[um] Francisco Eaton de Ciui[ta]te Bristoll
	Carpinter et Dorothie ux[ori] eius p[ro] term[ino]
N[oe] m[astc]r	septem an[nor]um Sol[vendum] iiij s. vj d, pro lib
at New England	[er]t[at]e Bristoll, cu[m] dupl[ici] appar[ello] etc
	[etera] et unu[cum] le sute teloru[m] p[er]tin[tem] ad
	art [em] le Carpinter p[re]d[icti]
In dorso	[John Morgan son of Edward Morgan late of the
Indent[ure;	City of Bristol 'sailer' deceased put himself appren-
[On the back	tice to Francis Eaton of the City of Bristol 'carpinter'
of the indenture]	and Dorothy his wife for the term of seven years to
	be paid 4s. 6d. for the livery of Bristol, with double
	apparel etc. and one weaver's 'sute' of tools belong-
	ing to the craft of 'le Carpinter' aforesaid.

The m[aste]r coven[au]nt[es] at thend of the said terme to convey to thapp[re]ntice & his heires foreu[er] 25 acres of land lyinge in New England in America & Alsoe to giue unto him 15 bushells of wheate he servinge him truly the terme of his app[re]ntiship.

15 (a) Appointment by Richard Lord Protector of the Sheriff of Norfolk, 1658

RICHARD Lord Protector of the Com[m]onwealth of England Scotland and Ireland and the Dominions and Territoryes thereto belonging TO all Dukes Earles Barons Knights Freemen and all others of the County of Norfolke greeteinge WHEREAS wee have com-[m]itted to John Creamer Esq[ui]r[e] the said County of Norfolke with the Appurtenances to keepe the same dureing our pleasure As in and by our Letters Patents to him thereof made is more fully conteyned WEE doe therefore comand and require you that in all things which belong to the said office of Sherriffe Yee bee ayding and assisting to the said John Creamer the pr[e]sent sherriffe of the said County of Norfolke IN TESTIMONY Whereof wee have caused these our Letters to bee made Patent[es] WITNES ourselfe att Westminster the thirtieth day of November in the yeare of our Lord God one thousand six hundred Fifty and Eight.

Lenthall Maydwell

27 (a) Register of St. Cuthbert, Bedford, 1672-73

Bapt[ised] Bettey ye dafter of John: Tely: June ye 11
Bapt[ised] Jane ye dafter of Thomas Chapman July ye 17
Bapt[ised] John ye soon of Thomas Watson octtobr ye 5
Bapt[ised] Joseph Bunyan ye son of John Bunyan Nov[ember] 16
Bapt[ised] Marey Dafter of Thomas Neller febray ye 6
Baptised Judy Scot dafter of John Scot Apr[il] 26: 1673.

27 (b) Bishop's transcript, Broughton Hacket, Worcs., 1683-84

Broughton   Transcriptio vera [true copy] An[no] Do[mini] 1684
Hagget
Sarah Rixon a poore trauelling woman was buryed the second day of Aprill.
Mary the daughter of Joseph Lacye al[ia]s Hobday & Fayth his wife was baptized the one & twentyth day of Aprill.

John Spilsbury of the p[ar]ish of St Martins in the Citye of Worcester & Winifrid Jenning of the same p[ar]ish were marryed the eighth day of June.

.   .   .   .   .

Roger Sanders Rect[or] Thomas Holliotte William Hunt Church
Wardens.

A Friendly caution to all Malsters, Millers, & other dealers in Corn.

Observe my woful case, & view it ovell
And learn from me to Buy as well as Sell
W-NG'd with too eager haste at getting gain.
J-ff-n J cheated, & ill treated P-yne,
L-ns-ll, & L-ke, & half a hundred more,
They all condemn me on the Roguish score
The parent Widow & her Offspring call
Aloud for vengeance on my head to fall,
The pig I forced to Market with my own
Scream'd out you Rascal all the way to Town
My odious Name has been so bad accounted
I'm thus degraded, & as ill am mounted.
My Foes I find they would not grudge the cost
To see me drench'd, or in a Blanket tost:
But see above my Just deserts appear
The pill'ry & the Gallows both are near

The Parish Pump, or The Miller's Tale

Lampoon in verse and drawing against a miller of Braintree, Essex, which was stuck on the pump in the Market Place. He faces and holds an ass's tail, his false measure around his neck; he stands in the pillory; the gallows awaits him. Mr Wing engaged William Grant, an attorney of Braintree, to sue the libelling author. Found in this attorney's album which also contained fulsome love letters, amorous verses, election pamphlets, his Will, etc.

[83]

VI

Extracts from
Selected Archives not Illustrated

Note. Capitals have been restricted to those in modern usage, and arabic numerals have replaced roman numerals.

1. *John Hill's charity accounts, Rowington, Warwickshire, 1553-4*

Payed for bread and wyne from my first accounte untyll we sett up the masse agayne, 3s. 2d.

Bestowed in the fowle wayes to men workyng carryeng gravell and for makynge the brydge at Shakesseperes, 41s.

For bread and ale to the carryars and workemen, 2s.

Delyvered to John Shaxspere forthe of the money whiche I had of Mr Baylie for Margett Cryar, 6s. 8d.

Waxe for the Sepulcre lyghtes and makyng the same, 8s. 5d.

Delt on good Frydaye to the pore, 6s. 8d.

For 3 quarters for John Hylles Obbyttes, 18d.

To the parishe clerke for a yere endyd at seynt Marye daye in lent in the first yere of the reigne of quene Marye, 2s.

To the constable toward the taske [tax], 9s. 2d.

For a new pyxe, 3s.

To the Commyssioners for certen churche goodes, 10s.

To the churchemen forthe of John Hylles wyll, 2s. 8d.

Payed for wrytynge up my counte, 4d.

For 2 tapers when we sett up the masse, 9d.

Summa of my payments, £4 17s. 2d.

2. *Churchwardens' accounts, St Margaret, Westminster, 1660–61*

Paid for ringing on the Coronation of King Charles the second, 20s.
To the towne weights for playing on the day of the Kings Coronation, 50s.
Delivered to them in bread and wine, 5s. 2d.
To Doctor Gifford for preaching of a sermon in this Church upon Sabboth day the 14th of Aprill 1661, 20s.
Paid for a coach to fetch him from Cornhill, 5s.
To severall porters which brought in the blew cloath into the Vestrie that the King walked uppon att his Coronation, 17s. 6d.
Paid to Henry Richards for making of a scaffold in the engine house to sett the hoggshead of wine uppon which rann at the Kings Coronation, 5s.
Paid for ringing on the day that the Kings Majestie rode to Parliament, 20s.
Paid for a hoggshead of French wine which runn at the Coronation of King Charles the second, £8.
Spent on a dynner uppon the Bishopp Almners Gentlemen that brought in the blew cloath which his Maiestie trode uppon att the day of his Coronation, 16s.

3. *Accounts of Surveyors of Highways, Winston, Co. Durham, 1699*

	£	s	d
For paveing 70 roods of cawsey at 1 shill: per rood	3	10	0
For ye bridge & cawsey in ye Long Lane on ye parish part	0	2	6
For drink for ye parishoners then & there	0	2	0
For part of a draught then & there	0	2	6
For 2 bowles of lime to ye bridge	0	1	6
For stubbing shrubs & whins in ye highway	0	1	0
For 6 roods more cawsey paving at 1^s per rood	0	6	0
For a warrant	0	0	6
Disbursed in all	4	06	0
Rec^d of ye parish half book of rates	4	01	10

4. *Accounts of Surveyors of Highways, Longburton, Dorset, 1768*

Paid Jas. Perrat for 27 feet of pavement att 1d. per foot	o	2	3
And for 6 load of walling stone	o	5	6
Paid John Down for work don in the street	o	4	4
Paid Joseph Brett for drawing of 68 load of stone att 4d. pr. load	1	2	8
And for 6 days work	o	6	o
Paid Abraham Parker for riting of Streat Lane gate and rayeling att Stockbridge gate	o	1	o
[And 5 similar payments for drawing and work]			
Jas. Perratt 3 days beer	o	o	6
[And further payments to workmen for beer]			
Paid for a presentment at privey sessions	o	o	6
Expenses att privey sessions	o	1	o
Total	3	10	5

5. *Overseers of the poor accounts, East Ham, Essex, 1782*

(As the burden of poor relief increased, entries of weekly payments filled many pages each year in the accounts of populous parishes. In addition, hundreds of tradesmen's and similar bills for workhouse and other supplies may be preserved, the totals only being given in the account-books.)

Paid for signing the rate-book, 2s. 6d.

Ynyr Burges Esq. for rent for the Almshouses, £2.

Bill to Messrs Scott and Willis due to the parish of St Giles, Colchester, for maintenance of John Mills wife and child, £9 9s. 11d.

Henry Taylor for Armstrong lodging, £1 7s.

Mr Davis his bill for expences at Chelmsford on the tryal of Barney Farrel [see no. 8 below], £3 9s. 9d.

Mr Davis a years salary as Parish Clerk, £2 10s.

Mr John Turner his bill for funerals, £7 14s.

Bridge Money [one of the County rates], £5 10s. 8d.

Mr Davis his bill for burying a poor man, 5s.

Mr Davis his bill for his Constables accounts, £6 12s. 7d.

Mr Nich. Carter one quarters rent for the Wedow Holloway, 11s. 3d.
[and seven similar payments for paupers' rents].

Mr Mizon his bill for funerals, £1 15s.
Wilson half a years salary as Vestry Clerk, £3.
Workhouse bill, £14 17s. 9d.

6. *Pauper examination, parish of St Martin-in-the-Fields, Westminster, 1709*

Elizabeth Dennis sayes she is the wife of James Dennis, a Black: she was marryd to him at Knightsbridge 22 yeare ago last October, by the name of Elizabeth Thistlewaite; her said husband then lived with Lord Chancellor Jefferys with whom he had lived about two yeare before she marryd, and my Lord Chancellor Jefferys then lived in St James Park in St Margaret, Westminster: and her said husband then was a servant to his Lordship – and now he lives with my lord Windsor at Chelsey. Sir Thomas Jefferys brought her husband from Spain and lodged with the Chancellor.

7. *Pauper examinations on settlement, Rainham, Essex*

(No. 6 is of unusual interest. No. 7 is a small selection of average interest from the church chest of a parish which is now in the London Borough of Havering. All examinations bear the signatures of the J.P.s before whom they were taken, and the signature (or mark) of the examinant.)

Settlement by apprenticeship, 1748. Joseph Lee of Rainham declareth that about 18 years ago he was bound an apprentice by indenture for 7 years to one John Baker of St Andrew Undershaft in Leadenhall Street in the City of London, peruke maker, and that he served the full term, and that he is lawfully married to his present wife Mary, by whom he has two children, Joseph aged 3 and Robert aged 1¾.

Settlement by renting house above value of £10 a year, 1770. Hugh Jones of Rainham, schoolmaster, saith that he was born (as he hath heard and verily believes to be true) in Wrexham in Denbighshire in Wales, and in 1759 and 1760 he hired a house at Uxbridge in the parish of Hillingdon in Middlesex at the yearly rent of £11, that he continued therein above one year, and in 1764 and the two succeeding years he let himself as a yearly assistant to Edward Ginger of Nantwich in Cheshire, schoolmaster, at the rate of £60 a year, and during that time he rented a house in Nantwich where he resided at the yearly rent of £5 and also land at £6, and that since that time he hath not done any act by which he hath gained a subsequent settlement elsewhere, and that he was lawfully married to Elizabeth his present wife, by whom he hath one daughter Laetitia aged near two years.

Settlement by birth, 1770. Robert Hayward of Rainham, blacksmith, saith that he was born in the parish of Hornchurch, that he hath worked with his father, whose name also is Robert, several years at the trade of a blacksmith, in the same house wherein he was born, that he enlisted into the 34th Regiment of King's Volunteers but cannot with certainty name the year or how long he continued therein but had his discharge from Patrick Tony, Colonel of the Regiment.

Settlement by hired service for a year (female), 1773. Ann Vantham, widow, saith that her husband George Vantham died about 12 years ago, and that she then hired herself as a yearly servant to Mr. Thomas Langley, a blacksmith at Rainham, at the wages of £4 a year, with whom she continued two years and received her full wages, and that she hath not since done anything whereby to gain a settlement elsewhere.

Settlement by hired service (male), 1832. Thomas Macdonnell, single man, complains before me that he can get work no where, altho' he has everywhere diligently sought it, and is therefore utterly poor and destitute and impotent to procure food and the other necessaries of life for himself. That he is now dwelling in Upminster, but believes himself to be settled in Rainham, for that 7 or 8 years ago he let himself after harvest time to Mr Thomas Simmons of Rainham Lodge for one year at the wages of £11 with lodging and board to serve him as cowman and stableman, that he continued without interruption to the end of his year and received all his wages and dwelt at Rainham Lodge, and that before and after this year's service he had worked with the said Mr Simmons for weekly wages connectedly and uninterruptedly with the said year's service.
[Added.] If this complainant speaks truth, and there appears no reason whatever to doubt his word, he is clearly settled at Rainham, and the officers there ought to find him work or otherwise relieve him, tho' by law they need not do so in the first instance but may put Upminster to the expense of relieving and removing him, which, considering that Mr Simmons is still living and comeatable, would be a very unworthy and unneighbourly dealing towards Upminster. [Folded and addressed by the J.P. 'To the Overseers of the Poor of the parish of Rainham'.]

8. *Vestry minutes, East Ham, Essex, 1739–1864*

(Vestry minutes, sometimes termed 'Parish books' or 'Town books', may be brief or detailed, covering almost every aspect of church and civil affairs, especially of course the work of the churchwardens, constables, surveyors of highways and overseers of the poor. The following are examples of unusual entries.)

24 April 1739. At a publick Vestrey held in the Parish Church of East ham it was unanimously agreed that Mr Arthur Bettesworth of London book seller and also parishoner and inhabitant of East ham should have leave to erect and build at his own proper cost and charge in the south west part of the church yard a vault or burying place for him self and family for ever exclusive of all others. [Signatures of vicar and 16 parishioners.]

15 Sept. 1782. It being represented that Richard Moss aged 14 years son of John Moss an old inhabitant of this parish returning homewards from the White Post on Sunday evening the 8th instant was attack'd by a footpad who demanded his money and afterwards wantonly and cruerly wounded and stabbed the said Richard Moss with a catlas of which wounds and stabs the said Richard Moss languished until Tuesday the 10th instand and then expired. And it being further repersented that from the description of the person and dress of the supposed murderer as given by the said Richard Moss there is sufficient evidence to suspect Barney Farrell a laborer to be the person who committed the said murder. This Vestry taking the above into consideration and to show their abhorance of such an uncommon act of cruelty and to make known their intention on all futuer occasions to prosecute such atrocious offenders do unanimously Resolve – That a reward of twenty guineas be paid to such person or persons as shall apprehend or give such information as may tend to the apprehending of the said Barney Farrell and that the Churchwardens be authorized to pay the same.

26 Feb. 1798. At a meeting of a Vestry at the Parish Church of Eastham call'd by genneral printed notice the Rev. John Lott Phillips in the Chair to consider the expediency of a Genneral Collection throughout this parish towards the Voluntary Contributions now receiveing at the Bank Resolved unanimously – That at a time when our religion, libertys and laws, and our verry existence as a free people are manest with distruction by an inveterate and ferocious enemy, truly sensible of the

blessings we enjoy under our present excellent constitution we are resolv'd to show our firm determination to resist them by every means in our power. Resolv'd therefore unanimously that books shall be opend for the purpose of receiving of Voluntary Subscriptions at the Cock at Eastham, the Green Man Plashet and at the Rising Sun on the Ilford Road and that after they have been open ten days a General Collection shall be made from house to house. Resolv'd unanimously that this resolution be printed in one or more dayly news papers and that their be a column open in each subscription book for every person to enter the sums they have subscribed in other parishes.

13 Jan. 1831. We the undersigned have inspected the Poor House of the parish of Barking and were perfectly satisfied with the good order and industrious habits introduced therein which confirm us in our opinion that farming the poor of the parish on the same principle is the best plan that can be adopted provided the same good order is observed here and continu'd [5 signatures].

6 May 1864. At a Special Vestry to take into consideration the large amount contributed by this parish towards the [West Ham] Union expenditure in proportion to the number of paupers as compared with the parish of West Ham, and further to take such steps as may be deemed necessary in conjunction with the parishes of Walthamstow, Wanstead, Woodford, Leyton and Little Ilford towards obtaining a separation from the parish of West Ham . . .

9. *Will of Samuel Barker of Prittlewell, Essex, tanner, 1639*

In the name of God Amen. [21 Feb. 1638/9.] I Samuel Barker of Prittlewell in the County of Essex tanner being sicke in body butt of good mind and perfect memory doe ordeyn and make this my last will and testament in manner and forme following. First I commend my soule into the handes of Almighty God my Maker trusting through the meritt of Christe his sonne to have my sinnes pardoned and my soule saved. And my body I comitt to the earth whence it was taken to be decently buryed att the discrecion of my executrix herin named. Imprimis I bequeath unto Elizabeth my wife my dwelling house with all the houshold stuffe whatsoever contayned in the same together with the orchardes gardens hopgroundes outhouses and all the appurtenaunces thereunto belonging to her and her heyres for ever. Item I bequeath unto Elizabeth my sayd wife two acres of ground more or lesse called Mill Croft lyeing in Prittlewell to her and to her heyres for ever. Item I give and bequeath unto Elizabeth my sayd wife all the hides, leather and skins whatsoever in my tanyard and the lease of my sayd tanyard together with my barke and horses. Item I give unto John Wittam the sonne of John Wittam of Northshoberry in Essex the sum of ten poundes to be payd unto him att the age of one and twenty yeares. Item I give unto my brother John Wittam and Frances his wife fourty shillings to be payd a yeare after my decease. Item I give unto Thomas Pecke vicar of Prittlewell fourty shillings to be payd a yeare after my decease. Item I give unto the poore people of Prittlewell fourty shillings. Item I give unto my two men John Peperill and George Richardson ten shillings a peice to be payd a year after my decease. Item I make Elizabeth my wife sole executrix of this my last will and testament and John Wittam of Northshoberry my brother overseer. In witnesse wherof I sett to my hand and seale the day and yeare abovewritten.

Sealed and delivered in the presence of us   Samuell Barker
Thomas Peck Tho. Cocke John Boys
[Added.] Memorandum that Elizabeth Barker my wife is to keep Hannah Barker my kinswoman for the rent of her house till she comes of age to enjoy it.
Probatum apud Chelmesford 14to Martii 1638 [proved at Chelmsford, 14 March 1638/9].

10. *Inventory of Andrew Myles of Bildeston, Suffolk, tanner, 1576*

In the haule one cupporde one framed table 2 chayers with serteyne stoles and with the stayned clothes 3 cusshyns a fyer panne a payer of tonnges and 2 littell cobberns and 3 tramells a payer of bellows one payer shyers a bottell pryse 26s. 8d.

In the chamber one posted bedd 2 flocke beddes a payer of blancketes 2 coveringes a boulster 4 pillows 5 curtayns with sarteyne stayned clothes 5 hutches a framed table one forme prise £3.

In lynnen 3 payer of sheetes 5 pyllowbeers 2 table clothes with other smaule lenen 13s. 4d.

In the butterye in pewter 22 peesses 9 pesses of brasse 2 lattyn candellstyckes one fryenge panne a lattyn chaffyngdisshe 2 spittes one trevett pryse 30s.

In another chamber one posted bedd one other beddstedd 2 flocke bedes 2 payer of blancketes 2 covrynges 2 boulsters one pyllowe one lyttle table one hutche a hamper and aulde stayned clothes pryse 26s. 8d.

In the tanne hawsse 2 hyedes one barke 4 calves skynnes one hogges skynne and hallfe a load of barcke 30s.

In the backehouse a payer of querns a mouldinge boord a payer of trestells 2 bowls a parser and a shave wedge with other tryeffles pryse 10s.

In the yard 2 lods of woode pryse 4s.

His apparell a payer of hoses a dublett a jurkyn an oulde cloke pryse 6s. 8d.

The sum is £10 7s. 4d.

[Names of seven appraisers.]

11. Inventory of William Gray of Alnwick, Northumberland, 1590

In my owne chamber wher I ly in, a turned trusinge bed corded with a teaster uppon the head and irones belonginge to it which the courtinges showld rune upon. A trunle bed corded a cubborde with the tressels and one iron chimney with loke and kye.

In the great chamber, a turned trusinge bede with a teaster one it of wood a hule bed corded a longe table with formes belonginge to it a chare two cubbordes one that the plat standes one and a nother that the virgenalles standeth on and a pare of virgenalles with locke and keye.

In Mr Bates chamber above, a trusinge bede corded a trunele bed corded a cubbord and the frame to stande upon with locke and keye.

In the litell chamber besides, on cubbord and a buffett stoole with loke and key.

In the gallery chamber, a trusinge bed corded with a teaster a bove it a cubbord with a frame locke and kye.

In the chamber above the hall, a turned trusinge bed corded with a teaster above head an other trusinge bed corded a litle round table with tresels locke and key.

In the brewhouse lofte, a copper kettell to be sette as a brewe lead.

In the lowe hall, a longe table and a short table with a frame with the formes belonginge to them and one iron chimney one ambrye carvede and shelves for vessells.

In the kitchine, 2 dressinge bordes with lock and keye.

In the brewhowse, in the bakeside on worte trowgh and a great stone trowghe to knocke corne in with locke and keye.

In the buttrey wher my wif lyeth, on cubbord ther in the manner of an ambery with locke and kye and one ambry with lockes and kyes.

[92]

12. *Inventory of the good and chattels of Jarvis Pyke of Merriott, Somerset, 1667*

His weareing apparrell, 10s.

In the Chamber over the Hall and in the other Chamber three bedsteeds with the beds and beding, £1 10s.; three coffers and a chest, 13s. 4d.

In the Hall a table board and frame and a cupboard, 13s. 4d.; one kettle and the pewter, £1 6s. 8d.; one brewing buckett, fower barrells, two payles and a tackboard, 12s.; a trendle, a little buckett, a gurnett, two turnes and a beame and scales, 10s.

A little mow of hemp, £2.

The valuacion of two acres of flax and flaxseed, £4; utensells belonging to the flax trade, 3s. 4d.

Nine stocks of bees, 18s.

A chattle lease of a small cottage or dwellinghouse scittuatt in Merriott, £3.

Triveall things forgotten or not seene, 1s. 6d.

     Richard Phelps, Robt. Frenche, Appraizers. £4 18s. 2d.

13. *Inventory of James Clarke of Blidworth, Notts., yeoman, 1699*

[In this and many other inventories archaic, obsolete or provincial terms or forms of words are often found. 'Landiron' = andiron; 'fould of fleaks' = (sheep) pen of wattled hurdles; 'huslements'= household goods. 'Cheesas' is not a misreading of chests: cf. Kitchen Chamber. See *Notts. Household Inventories*, ed. P. A. Kennedy (Thoroton Soc., Record Series, xxii, 1963) or similar local books, and generally the *Oxford Eng. Dict.* (13 vols., 1933).]

His purse and apparrell, £10.

In the house 2 tables 1 form 2 buffet stooles and 6 chaires £1 10s. 1 pair of verginals 11 pewter dishes with other pewter £4.

In the parlour 1 table 1 form 1 buffet stoole 7 leather chaires and half a dozen of cushans 1 carpet 1 livery cupbord 1 silver boule 2 silver spoones and other things £6 15s. 1 looking glass 10s.

In the great chamber 2 bedsteads and beding 8 chaires 3 chesas 1 box 2 dozen of napkins 2 tablecloths 2 pieces of woollen cloth 1 bunch of yarne with other things £19.

In another chamber 1 bed and beding 2 cheesas and 1 forme £2.

In the store chamber 1 table 2 cheesas 1 bacon flick and 10 cheesas £3.

In the kitchin chamber 2 bedsteads and 1 beding 1 cheeast £1 15s.

In the kitchin 3 brass pans 1 brass pot 2 iron pots 2 tubs 2 spits 1 land iron and other fire irons £4 10s.

In the booting house 2 kneading tubs and 1 churne 15s.

In the sellar 7 barrels 10s.

Corne in the chamber, £4. Hay in the barne £1.

6 acres of corn on the ground £12.

2 carts 2 plows 3 harrows and 1 fould of fleaks £8.

6 cowes 6 young bease 3 calves £30. 260 sheep £104. 2 swine £2.

4 mares and 2 foales and the horse geares £16.

Manure in the yard wheele timber and other huslements £5.

Sume totall £236 5s.

14. *View of frankpledge with court baron, three Warwickshire manors: extracts, 1581–1658*

Stoneleigh

5 Oct. 1581.

Every inhabitant thear shalbe contrybutory and paye the hyer to the molecatcher for takinge of wantes in the feyldes and meadowes thear accordinge to the rate of their landes upon payne of every of them refusinge so to doe to forfeyt 3s. 4d.

None of the inhabitants thear shall serve their swyne in troves or payles in the towne or comon streetes but shall provyde howsinge for the same in their backsydes or upon their owne groundes upon payne of forfeytinge 3s. 4d.

12 Apr. 1604.

The jurie shall walke the perambulation between Coventrie and Stonley with the inhabitantes upon the Assention even, to viewe and sett out the true markes and boundes.

No person shall kepe anie greyhoundes or other houndes or sett ginnes for destroyinge of hares within the precinct of this Mannor on paine everie defalte for everie weeke done without licence of the Lorde 10s.

A strict chardge was given that the cunstable shall every moneth call forth the inhabitantes to exercise Archery accordinge to the statute, signifienge that every one that is aged 7 yeares and so to 17 by the statute is to have a bowe and two arrowes, and from 17 to threescore to have a bowe and fower arrowes, and to exercise the same, not being lame or unable.

Henley-in-Arden

5 Apr. 1592.

Noe person shall here after shuete in any hand gonne, crose bowe or

[94]

stone bowe within the precyncte of this manor at any pyggyns uppon payne to forfeyte 3s. 4d.

11 Oct. 1592.

No victuler viz. aylehowse kepers within this maner shall suffer any cardes, tables, shovlebourde to be used within their howses or any company to remayne drinkinge att service time eyther at morninge or eveninge prayer excepte travelours on paine to forfeite 3s. 4d.

8 Oct. 1596.

Noe inhabitant within this libertie shall laye mucke, dust or any other drosse in the backe lane from John Parkers howse to the Crosse nor likewise any blockes or wood in the streete to the disturbance of the people upon payne to forfett 2s.

5 Oct. 1597.

We agree that yf any above thage of 12 yeres doe suit [shoot] in any pece, fowlinge pece, birdinge pece or suche like within this libertie to forfeit his pece and forfeit £10 to the lord of the mannor.

4 Oct. 1598.

Whoesoever within the libertie shall abuse the Baylief by evell demeanors shall forfait therefore unto the Lord of the Manor 40s.

All those which buy wood of hedg tearers or stealers of wood shall forfait 3s. 4d. And they that shall sell it to be putt in prison and there remaine 24 howers.

20 Oct. 1615. Presentments.

A bloodshed mad by twoo of Sir William Sommerfeilds men viz. the Butler and the Fawkener (2s. apece) uppon John Collier. The men I did not see nether there names I doo not knowe.

21 Oct. 1618.

We present Elizabeth Smith the wife of Thomas Smith cutler for a common scolde. Ideo subeat penam lavandi super le cookingstoole

Weapens forfeted. Twelve men finde on sworde of Wineates that he did breake the pease on Christopher Tup and the same sworde praised at 1s.

Peter Maunton kepeth a mault querne and taketh in mault to grynd in hinderance of the Lordes mill, yet the Lord is contented to forbeare any fyne or amercement for this court onely.

20 Oct. 1619.

Twelve men present Thomas Lacye (10s.) for givinge Mr. Baylyfe unmannerly wordes videlicet Knave, and present Elner Powell for that she is a scold and liveth unquietly. Judgment that she shalbe cooked [set in the cooking-stool].

Franciscus Yonge et Alicia uxor eius (Francis Y. and Alice his wife) hath stolen one flagon, six pewter dishes, one paire of wollen cardes. Judicium Curie [The Court's judgment] that they shalbe both whipped.

Alveston

5 Oct. 1655. Presentments.

Thomas Higgins for a pound breach, therefore hee is amerced 6s. 8d.

Thomas Dennet Constable for not providinge a paire of stockes accordinge to the statute, amerced 1s.

15 Oct. 1658.

Richard Baker for takeinge in and continuinge an inmate contrarye to the statute and amerce him 12d.

William Godwin for erectinge and continuinge two cottages and amerce him 4s.

Walter Millard (2d.) and Thomas Compton (2d.) for neglectinge watch and ward.

They present the parish of Alveston and the inhabitants and parishioners thereof for wateringe of hemp and flaxe and unlawfull fishinge in the river of Avon and for doeinge other nusances in the water there. Therefore amerced 6s. 8d.

15. *Court leet (penalties), manor of Brassington, Derbys., 1663*

Pains agreed by the Great Inquest at the Court Leet [9 May 1663].

That everyone everie yeare make his common yates att or before the five and twentieth daie of March or else to forfeit for everie yate not made and kept in good and sufficient repaire to forfeite, 18d.

Everie man everie year make his ring fences about the Pastures in good and sufficient repaire att or before the five and twentieth daie of March or else to forfeit 18d.

Everie one everie yeare scowre their ditches adjoyneinge to the Kings highway before the first daie of May or else to forfeite 12d.

Noe person shall wash clothes, beastes meate, or swines meat or any noysome or filthy thinge att the Coole Well or other wells in the towne within three or foure yardes of the wells mouthes to corrupt the water to forfeit uppon payne for everie default 12d.

Noe myner shall carry either on horse or otherwise water from the

Coole Well or common wells aforesaid to wash oare or ould hillocks in the liberty or att their houses uppon payne to forfeit 12d.

Everie man who shall keepe any swine unringed every week he neglects shall for every swyne forfeite 3d.

If any person be taken breakeing fences or cutting any wood that is not their owne or pullinge downe the pasture walls unlawfully shall forfeit, 18d.

If any person doe not keepe up their rams from the fourth daie of September till the tenth daie of October shall forfeite 12d.

No person shall sheate or course any mans sheepe on the Common Pasture to hurte or beate them upon payne 12d.

Whosoever shall take in any inmate without giving security to the officers of the Towne of Brassington aforesaid shall forfeite 20s.

No person shall digge or delve anie turves to carry them out of the liberty haveing no privilege on the Common for everie default to forfeite 3s. 4d.

Noe person shall putt any beast above his stente on the Pastures not haveinge a beast gate shall forfeite 3s. 4d.

If any person shall neglect to paie the pynners wages after twoe pence a beaste (as a due to him) shall forfeite for everie beast 4d.

16. *Court leet and court baron, manor of Mansell Lacy, Herefs., 1654*

Manner of Maunsell Lacey. The Courte Leete and Courte Baron of James Rodd Esquier and John Tailor Gent. held [20 April 1654] before Edward Alderne Dr of Lawes Steward there.

Essoines [i.e. excuses for non-attendance] [7 persons, named].

Homage [i.e. the jurors] [12 persons, named].

The jury do present John Harper for beatinge and abusinge the Lords bayliefe and doe fine him in 6d. and to bee paid before the next Courte.

The jury do present [4 men, named] for keepinge of goates and if they keepe them longer than Michaelmas next they impose a paine of fower pence weekely upon them.

The jury doe appoint Arthur Hill and William Brewne overseers of the highways and the said wayes to bee amended and made lawfull before the fower and twentieth of June and doe fine every teeme holder in 12d. and every other inhabitant who are lyable to the duty if they make defalt in 4d.

The jury doe present the want of a pound and stocks in theyr parish and doe consent that the said pound and stocks bee made by the second day of August and that the said parish to be at the charge of makeinge and that the said tymber bee had by the Lords appointment before the 14th day of May next.

17. *Letter from John Wesley, Bristol, 1748*

Bristol, Feb. 12, 1747–8

At my return from Ireland, if not before, I believe the School in Kingswood will be opened. If your son comes there, you will probably hear complaints; for the discipline will be exact: it being our view, not so much to teach Greek & Latin, as to train up soldiers for Jesus Christ. I am obliged now to go the shortest way to Holy-head, my brother being almost impatient for my arrival. I am sorry to hear that Mr Thomas thinks of leaving Mr Hedges: I doubt their separation will not be for the furtherance of the Gospel. My love and service attend all your family. I am,

Your affectionate friend and servant,

John Wesley.

18. *Diary of a Clitheroe, Lancashire, weaver, 1864*

April 10. The American war seems as far of [f] being settled as ever. The mill I work in was stopped all last winter, during which time I had three shillings per week allowed by the relief committee, which barely kept me alive. When we started work again it was with Surat cotton and a great number of weavers can only mind two looms. We can earn very little. I have not earned a shilling a day this last month and there are many like me. My clothes and bedding is wearing out very fast and I have no means of getting any more as what wages I get does hardly keep me after paying rent, rates and firing. I went twice to Preston to see my brother Daniel, but him and his family were no better off than myself, having nothing better than Surat to work at, and it is the same all through Lancashire.

19. *Mining lease, Camborne, Cornwall, 1825*

(Abstract of 'sett' for 21 years, for one-twelfth of the profits, giving licence to 'dig, work, mine and search for tin, copper and lead in Kellyhellan, Camborne, west on course of Wheal Rome lode, east on same lode to join lands of Lord de Dunstanville and Basset, north of the lode 200 fathom and south 100 fathom'. Lessee may make new shafts, erect buildings and machines; tin to be spalled and rendered fit for stamping, other minerals to be dressed and made merchantable. Lessee to make a division once every six months and to give lessor notice of this and of every ticketing, also to give him once a year a full plan and section of the mine and of all lodes and veins discovered. Lessee to work according to 'the rules and practice of good miners' and to keep shafts open with timber props and in good repair, to leave soil removed in heaps and to fence off shafts. When shafts cease to be worked lessee to fill up or 'sufficiently sollar the same'.

['Sett', lease stating boundaries and terms of the ground taken by mining adventurers. 'Lode', regular vein producing any kind of metallic ores. 'Spall', to break the rock from the ore. 'Stamping', process of crushing ores and by use of water to take away waste particles, leaving black tin (it was called white tin after smelting). 'Division', financial settlement. 'Ticketing', sale of ores (for smelting) by tender. 'Sollar', covering shaft.])

20. *Minutes of Epping and Ongar Turnpike Trust, Essex, 1773, 1816*

(Contract for £360 with John Glyn for road improvement at Golden's Hill in Loughton, May 1773.)

He will sink the said hill 16 feet perpendicular opposite to the corner of the wall of Richard Clay Esq. next to the 'Red Lion' and will raise the same at least 16 feet at the bottom of the said hill opposite to the 'Plume of Feathers', and make the same road with the most easy declivity that may be from opposite the 'Shoe Maker' to the corner below the wheeler's shop at the bottom of the dell, and to finish the said work by 30th day of October.

January 1816. Tolls authorized:	s.	d.
If drawn by more than 2 horses	1	0
For every waggon or wain drawn by 6 horses or less	1	6
For every waggon or wain drawn by more than 6 horses	2	0
Every limber carriage drawn by 3 or more horses or mules	2	0
And if with less	1	6
For every mare, gelding, mule, horse, or ass not drawing		1
For neat cattle by the score		10
For calves, swine, sheep, or lambs by the score		5

And for every waggon, wain, cart, or carriage, except carts drawn by one horse only, having the fellies of the wheels thereof of less breadth or gauge than six inches from side to side at the least at the bottom, and for the horse or beast of draught drawing the same, double the tolls.

21. *Minutes of Guardians of the Poor, Bridgwater Union, Somerset, 1837*

(John Bowen of Bridgwater published a pamphlet (*The Reform Poor Law, with some account of its working on the Bridgwater Union*) which appeared in *The Times*, 21 July 1837, making allegations of oppression and neglect against the Board. They were investigated by the Board on 4 August at which an Assistant Poor Law Commissioner and 43 Guardians attended (extracts 1 and 2). Extract 1 forms part of the lengthy evidence of John Chinn, one of the Relieving Officers, concerning the specific case of Robert Kidner which formed part of Bowen's allegations: Kidner, his wife and four children had been admitted to the workhouse in December 1836; Kidner 'escaped' on 15 January and after 'fencing with the Board' up to 9 March was summoned before the local magistrates and committed to gaol for a month for refusing to maintain his family. The three committing J.P.s were Guardians and included the chairman and a former deputy chairman. The Board passed a unanimous resolution approving the J.P.s' action. Extract 2 is from the evidence of James Gover, the governor of the house, in so far as it bears on Bowen's charges. Extract 3 is from the minutes of 18 August, to which the inquiry was adjourned, and includes evidence of the matron and an inmate, Harriet Bindon. After hearing her evidence the Board stopped the inquiry and decided that the allegations against itself were unfounded, but Bowen returned to the attack in 1838.)

1. Kidner stated that he had no place to take them [his family], that his goods had been seized for rent; he was also offered before his committal to be allowed to go back into the Workhouse with his wife and family, which he also refused, stating that he preferred going to Gaol; he was then committed for one month to hard labour . . John Chinn then stated that Kidner had complained to him of the diet of the House not being sufficient to support him, but that he did not make any such complaint before the Magistrates at the time of his committal.
2. The Governor stated that a complaint had been made to the Board in February last, accusing him of not having supplied the things ordered by the Medical Officer to the sick paupers in the North Pether-

ton Workhouse, his answer was that he had not received an order from the Medical Officer to do so, nor had he seen the Medical Report Book, but supplied it immediately on receiving directions from the Board. On referring to his books he stated that he had sent tea, sugar and butter to the North Petherton Workhouse on 16th and 22nd February. Mr Poole Surgeon was sent for, who deposed that he had on several occasions in the last year attended on the Poor in the Workhouse for Mr Abraham King, who was then Medical Officer, that he attributed the sickness that prevailed in the House to the Dietary that was then used, but that he did not make any statement in writing to the Board to that effect, but that he had stated his opinion to the Visiting Committee.

3. That gruel was in her opinion wholesome food in the proportion given according to the late dietary. That the Poor in the North Petherton Workhouse never suffered any inconvenience for want of necessaries being supplied, if any delay had ever been occasioned, she had supplied trifles such as biscuits, tea and sugar herself . . . Harriet Bindon was called before the Board, and deposed that she was an inmate of the North Petherton Workhouse, that she was in February in ill health, she took to her bed soon after she came there, she was attended during her illness by Mr Tilsley, who told her that he had ordered tea, sugar and butter for her. Mr Tilsley on visiting her two days after and finding that they had not been supplied gave her some himself, they were from that time regularly supplied to her during the whole of her illness. She further stated that she was sent to North Petherton from the Bridgwater Workhouse, where she had been for some time before, that she was well treated when there, but that she could have eaten a little more food in her work than she had got.

22. *Minutes of Stratford-upon-Avon Board of Health, Warws, 1864–71*

30 March 1864. Ordered that the Police be empowered to barricade and prevent obstructions in the Streets during the Tercentenary Celebration and so as to fully carry out the provisions of the Towns Police Clauses Act 1847 under the direction of the Chairman of the Board.

27 July 1864. Read the monthly report of the Surveyor and Inspector of Nuisances. Ordered that the application of Mr Samuel Wilson relative to his Lodging House be granted; that the application of Mr Edgar

Flower to form a cellar way underneath the footpath in Pound Lane be refused, but that his application to pave the footpaths in Pound Lane and Greenhill Street with blue Bricks be granted, subject to the Pavement being taken up and removed in the event of the Town being repaved; that the Clerk see Mr Callaway relative to terms for keeping in order the Island formed in the River Avon.

25 Oct. 1865. It appearing to the Board from the report of two Medical Men to the Board of Guardians that Fever is prevalent in the Town, Ordered that notice be given that the Board have directed the Inspector of Nuisances at his discretion to supply any poor person in the District on his or her application with sufficient lime and the use of a Bucket and Brush free of Cost for the purpose of whitewashing the inside of the dwelling house of such poor person.

25 July 1866. Permission having been given by the Lady of the Manor to take down the Pound upon condition that the Board obtain a suitable place to deposit the Town Manure, Ordered that when the Surveyor has found a suitable place for the purpose aforesaid that the Pound be taken down.

26 Sept. 1871. Read a requisition signed by 13 inhabitants of the Town calling the attention of the Board to a Nuisance highly prejudicial to health arising from certain noxious effluvia issuing from a Chimney upon the premises of Mr Frederic Kendall [drug manufacturer] of High Street in the Borough of Stratford-upon-Avon and trusting that the Board would give the matter their early and serious consideration. Resolved that the Chairman be requested to call upon Mr Kendall and state that unless he will undertake to remove the Nuisance in one month the Board will cause an information to be laid against him before the Justices.

23. *Minutes of South Cave and Wallingfen Local Board, East Riding, Yorks., 1875–85*

Report of Medical Officer, 28 June 1875.
The first case of Diphtheria occurred in November 1874 in the house of Mr B. Lamb. The disease assumed a mild form so that in the course of a few days the young Lad got well.
The second and third broke out in the Village of Bromfleet. One

recovered in the usually short time and though the other a child of two years rallied for a time symptoms of Croup set in and proved fatal in a few hours.

The fever case occurred at Bromfleet Landing and was imported from Low Drewton.

Every precaution, I believe, was taken to prevent the spread of the disease and luckily in each instance the other Members of the Family escaped.

Now Gentlemen with regard to the Cause. In the solitary instances to which I have alluded I am unable to assign it to any special or local cause and am therefore driven to the conclusions that as disease and death are the lot of all Men I must submit and leave this question unanswered.

9 June 1879. Ordered that the Clerk do put up a notice on the black-smith's shop at Bromfleet that the Wallingfen Local Board propose to close the Watering Dike entirely as a place at which horses and cattle may be watered and washed and to put it into a good sanitary condition for the inhabitants to obtain their drinking water and requesting parties having objection to communicate with the Clerk.

21 March 1884. The only epidemic has been a slight outbreak of small pox on the Hull and Barnsley Railway at Weedley.

Report of Inspector of Nuisances, April 1885.
I had heard that the Privy belonging to the Schoolmaster's house was too near his dwellinghouse but your Medical Officer informed me that it is never used.

24. *Minutes of Ottery St Mary Highway Board, Devon, 1880*

April 26. The Surveyor's Report was read. With regard to certain nuisances at Newton Poppleford caused by occupiers allowing refuse, filth and foul water and drainage water into the watertroughs, and a like complaint of certain places at Rockbeare, the Clerk was directed to serve the usual notices on the occupiers so offending to abate the nuisance. With regard to the damage done to the roads in Sidbury by 'extraordinary traffic' caused by carriage of material from the building of the mansion now in course of erection by the Right Hon. Sir Stephen Cave, the Clerk was directed to write to his Agent giving the amount of claim as set forth in the Surveyor's Report.

25. *School Managers' log book, Loughton British School, Essex, 1866–70*

(The first and last of the reports on this school by Matthew Arnold as H.M. Inspector of Schools.)

27 July 1866. The discipline needs watchfulness but the Master who is efficiently assisted by his wife is now in my opinion working the school very well. The children appear to be much attached to him and the failures in the examination are remarkably and creditably few.

30 May 1870. The present Master, an old Pupil Teacher of mine, came here in July last. Both the attendance and the instruction have during the winter been greatly affected by scarlet fever, but the numbers are now considerable. The order is satisfactory. The cause of illness being removed, the weakness of the instruction, now far too great, must be remedied. The Arithmetic is defective all through the school and the spelling in the third and fourth Standards. The answering in Geography is good and this subject is taught in a way to interest the children. A competent person attends every afternoon to teach the Girls needlework. The water is not yet laid on to the offices. The Maps want renewing, and they should be hung up in the schoolroom.

My Lords will look for improvement as the condition of an unreduced Grant another Year. (Article 52 (a).)

VII

Appendix

Brief Note on Publications and Articles

THE LOCAL HISTORIAN

Quarterly, annual postal subscription £1·50, from the National Council of Social Service, for the Standing Conference on Local History, 26 Bedford Square, WC1. Issues before 1964 out of print but can be seen in most public libraries. This journal has many articles which are helpful to those using local archives.

HISTORY

Three times a year, annual subscription £2·50, from Historical Association, 59A Kennington Park Road, London SE11. This included in each issue 1962–7 a four-page article in its *Short Guide to Records* series; for example: 'Rate Books', 'Poll Books', 'Probate Inventories', 'Estate Maps and Surveys', 'Guardians' Minute Books', 'Chantry Certificates', 'Hearth Tax Records', 'Episcopal Visitation Books', 'Estate Acts of Parliament', 'Wills', 'Recusant Rolls', 'Deeds of Title'.

BRITISH RECORD SOCIETY'S INDEX LIBRARY
(86 volumes, in progress)

This is a key primarily to biographical and genealogical material (nearly one million names) and indirectly to social and economic history. Most volumes list wills and administrations of cities of London and Bristol. Each volume has an index of parishes under counties. The Society should not be confused with the British Records Association – its offspring, now much larger than its parent – nor with the List and Index Society, recently formed to print P.R.O. Lists and Indexes.

The reader is reminded that some of the most useful publications dealing with Local History are on pp. 6–9. It is unnecessary in this book to give a further list as this has been done by the Historical Association in the revised (1965) edition of *The English Local History Handlist: A Short Bibliography and List of Sources for the Study of Local History and Antiquities*, ed. F. W. Kuhlicke and F. G. Emmison, 43p post free.

Index

Text, transcripts and extracts - page numbers.
Illustrations - plate numbers in **bold** type.